I0486206

The Achilles Heel;

The IRS Notice of Federal Tax Lien

By H. Skip Robinson

Copyright Certificate of Registration Number:
TXu-1-945-343

Effective Date: November 2, 2014 in accordance with Title 17, United States Code.

ISBN 10: 1517797829
ISBN 13: 9781517797829

Dedications

This book is dedicate to all those who have fought tirelessly over the years and centuries in an attempt to restrain the overreaching confiscatory activities of the now estimated 87,576 different governments of the United States; a multi-level hierarchy of bureaucracies that make up the local, State and the Federal political conclaves of America.

Those such as Robert Schulz, Eustace Mullins, Peter and Irwin Schiff, the folks at the Independence Institute, Foundation for Economic Education, Joe Bannister, G. Edward Griffin, Sherri Jackson, Bill Benson, Bob Podolsky, Red Beckman, Melvin Stamper, Peter Hendrickson, Ted McAnlis, Harry Brown, Ron Paul, all the libertarians that have influenced my life, and those noted in the Chapter; Winners and Losers Against the IRS. And this is just a short list.

The Authors, many who are also noted above but others such as the brilliant Frederic Bastiat, Thomas Jefferson, Thomas Paine, Milton, Rose and their son David Friedman, Friedrich Hayek, Ludwig von Mises, Murray Rothbard, Charles Adams, Adam Smith, Jacob Hornberger, Thomas DiLorenzo, Charles Murray, Richard Ebeling, Henry Haslitt, and many others to help me gain the required knowledge to support this endeavor with all my heart and soul.

A very warmest and special thanks to my dearest Debi Trindade, my kids Matt and Chelsea, friends like Mark Stufft who tries to keep me in the fairway, Bill Tinnerman, Randy White, Jeff Pollard, Rory Leinen, Ken Snyder, Bob Koch, John Ellis, Wayne Harley, Gloria Hicks and all the others who have also helped me in so many ways.

Table of Contents

Chapter 1...1

Introduction 1

    The Presumption of Innocence 3

    Dominant Issues At Large: 11

Chapter 2...12

Material Evidence;..13

The Erroneous NFTL 13

    Summary of Material Evidence 31

Chapter 3...34

Evidence of Required Elements (NFTL) 34

    Subject Arrangement of Statutes:..................................36

    Various "Kinds of Tax" 42

    Other Kind of Tax Types and Subtypes 43

    Conclusion - Material Evidence....................................52

Chapter 4...54

Circumstantial Evidence; 54

We The People v. United States 54

    The Terms "State" and "United States" Defined 56

    Assumptions about Collection Fraud.............................63

    Title 26 is "Not" Positive Law......................................64

    About the United States Code from: 65

    THE TERM "POSITIVE LAW" 67

    What WE Know:..69

Chapter 5...71

Me and The IRS; never an answer 71

    Legal Analysis, 16th Amendment...................................78

    Conclusion from Circumstantial Evidence....................79

Chapter 6..83

Words, Terms and Case Histories 83

    Definitions: 83

    The Oath of Office..83

    Jurisdiction Explained 84

    Citizenship - Two Different Types? 86

    and important 14th Amendment Cases; 86

    "An Unlimited Power to Tax, a Power to destroy"..........89

Chapter 7..91

Winners and Losers against the IRS 91

Chapter 8..98

Arguments Against this Analysis...98

    The 16th Amendment...98

    The Income Tax Act of 1913 99

    & the Victory Tax of 1942..99

Chapter 9...102

Notice and Case for Fraud and Treason...............................102

    Purpose and Intent of the Notices 109

    Notice to the Proper Authorities 110

    Affidavit for Notice 111

Chapter 10..113

Additional Comments 113

    Overview of Income Tax History 117

    Sources of Information/ Bibliography 123

    LEGAL DISCLAIMER 125

CHAPTER 1
INTRODUCTION

The Tax Honesty Movement, named by its supporters and many groups, have been claiming for years that there is no Federal Statute (Law), that requires most Citizens, those within the 50 States of the United States of America to file and thus pay a Federal Personal/Individual Income Tax on their labor, when in an individual capacity. This will be explored later but this is **not** the issue of the material and circumstantial evidence and facts being evaluated and presented in this book.

What this book will show, by the material and circumstantial evidence provided, is that the IRS is issuing erroneous Notice of Federal Tax Liens and thus these invalid and legally insufficient liens are being filed by the various Clerks of Court around the Country, creating a fraudulent lien against those individuals. These liens are then used by the IRS, the Treasury Department, and Department of Justice to confiscate money and property by illegal enforcement methods from Citizens of the United States. If the Liens are legally insufficient they are by default, illegally enforcing them.

It is important to comprehend just how difficult it is to research and understand the Internal Revenue Code. The Internal Revenue Code (IRC) is over 9,450 pages long and is a codification, much like a desk reference manual. It entails all the tax laws ever enacted through the legislative process by Congress, so it encompasses all the estimated eighty (80) different types of taxes that Congress has enacted over 235 + years, that the Federal Government enforces and collects. The IRC indices (Table of Contents) alone are over 550 pages long.

Taxation and the voluminous amounts of law and judicial decisions are extremely complicated, with over two millenniums of enactments and hundreds or perhaps even thousands of important court cases on the various topics from, who is liable, to what is the definition of "Income". Not only that, but the issues involved like jurisdiction, citizenship, Federalism and States Rights and how they play a role in each tax and its enforcement.

If a law doesn't exist, how would you prove it does? Just as you can't prove a negative, you cannot prove a law doesn't exist. It is up to the claimant to do that, i.e. the Federal Government in this case, to prove that one exists. It is reasonable to conclude that the Government should provide the taxpayers the specific Federal Statute(s) and show when they were passed, but as you will come to understand, they will not. However, the issue of "does a law exist" is only some of the circumstantial evidence that helps to support the material evidence. I believe it shows the reason why the Notice of Federal Tax Liens being used to enforce the Federal Individual Income Tax are invalid and why the Government does not and more importantly cannot note the correct Kind of Taxes on the liens.

Government always has a propensity to increase taxes if it can get the Citizens to go along with it, even if some dissention exists, and the Judiciary has historically been a rubber stamp for centralized policy making, even going back to the very beginning of our democratic Republic, but most notably after the Civil War.

"The result is that a prejudgment garnishment of the Wisconsin type may, as a practical matter, drive a wage-earning family to the wall. Where the taking of one's property is so obvious, it needs no extended argument to conclude that, absent notice and a prior hearing this prejudgment garnishment procedure violates the fundamental principles of due process. For a poor man and whoever heard of the wage of

*the affluent being attached? -- to lose part of his salary of-
ten means his family will go without the essentials. No man
sits by while his family goes hungry or without heat. He either files for consumer bankruptcy and tries to begin again
or just quits his job and goes on relief. Where is the equity,
the common sense, in such a process?"* - Sniadach v. Family Finance Corp., 395 U.S. 337, 349

As you will soon understand, at least from my perspective, taxation is a game of the wealthy, through political cronyism, to take as much money from the majority of people as they can, without their revolt.

The Presumption of Innocence

The IRS is the only entity is the entire United States of America that operates under the premise that it does "not" require a "Court Order" to confiscate money or property from individuals, businesses or non-profit organizations. As you will come to understand, certain members of the Administration, all of Congress and certain members of the Judiciary are complicit in the abrogation of the Constitutional mandate of Due Process.

The IRS simply makes a claim of assessment, files a Notice of Federal Tax Lien and the debtor is subject to property, bank account and wage confiscation. There is a procedural system in place but even a Taxpayer's Bill of Rights does not really help you, as you will come to understand. Each process is just correspondence and alleged hearings with the participants from the government acting as a Kangaroo Court. If you try to challenge the system you will either be ignored or forced to expend huge sums of money on Attorneys, often times in a fruitless attempt to protect your property and wages.

Amendment V. No person shall….. be deprived of life,
liberty or property without due process of law.

As you will see, just because there is a process, this does not guarantee that justice will be served by that process. The information in this book is provided to show the Citizens of the United States how the IRS has been misleading people in the collection and enforcement of Federal Individual Income Taxes. For those of America within the Internal Revenue Service (IRS), the Departments of Justice and Treasury and the various County Clerks of Court around the country that do not know, they need to be appraised and "Officially Notified" that the Notice of Federal Tax Liens they are issuing and recording in the various Official County Records are legally insufficient and therefore invalid.

Ninety-nine (99%), of the Notices of Federal Tax Liens being issued by the IRS and being filed in the various County Court records are legally insufficient as lawful liens, according to the Federal government's own rules and regulations. They are legally insufficient because they lack specificity as to the correct Kind or Type of Tax being assessed, levied and enforced, contrary to Federal Statutes. As you will come to understand, this makes them invalid as legal liens. Most often times the IRS is erroneously noting the incorrect Sections of the Internal Revenue Code, as to the specific Kind of Tax, perhaps in a deceptive manner or just from ignorance of what the laws state.

It is not only common sense but well established law that the claimant or any taxing authority must note the correct Kind of Tax being imposed and enforced, providing their authority and jurisdiction, for any tax lien to be valid. The Internal Revenue

Service collects multiple kinds of taxes and who are liable for those taxes often differ as to both Citizenship type and Jurisdictions/locations. As an example, if you're a Citizen and resident of Puerto Rico you have a different tax liability than a Citizen and resident of the District of Columbia or the 50 States. As you will see later, most Citizens of Puerto Rico are not required to file and pay a Federal Individual Income Tax unless they receive income from outside of Puerto Rico. Most Citizens that earn money from working in Puerto Rico are not liable for a Federal Individual Income Tax on their employment.

Consider this, if the Notice of Federal Tax Lien does not correctly note the Kind of Tax that you owe them, then how can you possibly know if you're liable for the Tax they are assessing against you. As Citizens of a society based on liberty and justice for all, we cannot and should not just assume the enforcement of a tax is correct without the ability to know specifically which law or laws we are being forced and/or coerced through intimidation or threats of incarceration, to obey by the inferring tax being assessed and levied against us. Sadly, as you will learn, that appears to be the situation.

You will additionally come to understand some of the reasons of how the Federal Government has been getting away with this activity for so long and see how some of those in power have abrogated the Constitution to do it. The 1st Amendment "Right" and its recent abrogation in January 2008 to Petition the Government for Redress of Grievances will be closely examined.

That, by definition is an Act of Treason for those participants that are knowingly involved in the fraud. When those within the body politic knowingly and maliciously abrogate the foundation and intent of the Rule of Law, in this case the "Constitution" as a means of "taking" money or property, without reasonable due process, that is theft and treason and one could make the case that this is an act of "insurrection". Those in power have literally over-thrown our duly Constituted Government and replaced it with one with no lawful authority. What good is a Constitution if those in power can ignore it to usurp the rights and property of the Citizens and embrace it when needed to protect their own self-interests from prosecution or impeachment?

A large percentage of our population's money and property are literally being manipulated and controlled by bureaucrats and politicians, such as Dick Cheney, a career politician and bureaucrat, now worth an estimated $90 million dollars today.

*Title 28 §§ 2461 - 2465. In § 2463: "All property taken or detained under any revenue law of the United States shall **not** be repleviable, but shall be deemed to be in the custody of the law and subject only to the orders and decrees of the courts of the United States having jurisdiction thereof". (June 25, 1948, Ch. 646, 62 Stat. 974.)*

As the above Statute notes, it appears that the IRS does have the legal authority to take property, despite the previously noted Constitutional limitations of such an action protected under Amendment V. Once they have your money, *you* however do need a court order to get it back, which is almost impossible to do. The government does not need a court order to take your money but you need a court order just to get back what is rightfully yours. Of course the government has an endless pile of money to enforce or defend their actions and those with the money *to* fight back have much to lose in taking such risks.

This is what is called an "abrogation" of the Constitution. Politicians and Judges in 1948, just took it upon themselves to change/alter the intent and the protections of due process afforded the Citizens by the 5th Amendment of our Constitution and Bill of Rights. And they did this unlawfully, as they do have a means of properly/legally altering the Constitution. However it is quite difficult to even initiate a Constitutional Amendment and thus why bother if you can just change the law, like they did and get away with it. Especially when one considers the Courts are a party to the abrogation.

Sadly, this is just one of many abrogations of our Constitution over the years but obviously an important one. I will point out later in the book, a couple of other important abrogations specific to the income tax.

As you will see the IRS will not under any circumstances, ever tell you the specific Federal Statute/Tax Law that gives them the authority and/or applicable jurisdiction(s) they are operating under. Under Title 28 § 2461, any taking must be authorized by an Act of Congress and as you will discern for yourself, it appears Congress has never enacted an income tax that requires Citizens of the several 50 States to file and pay an Individual Federal Income Tax **on their labor, in their individual capacity**. There are a few caveats to this and these will be discussed later, but they do not apply to most people. However, this book does **"not"** focus on the Constitutionality of the Federal Income Tax or if Government can or cannot confiscate property without due process because it can and does, or if its enforcement is even constitutional. Those issues are important and will be examined but only as circumstantial evidence to give the reader a broader understanding of taxation, its enforcement and the primary focus of this book.

What this book does focus on, is if the tens of thousands of people issued Notices of Federal Tax Liens (NFTL) by the Internal Revenue Service (IRS), is whether these liens are valid instruments with the statutorily required specific details and content for them be to legally sufficient and therefore enforceable as tax liens in a court of law.

Consider the potential of the IRS, Treasury, prosecutors and Judges having to acknowledge that these Liens are invalid.

As you will see, the IRS does not appear to be able or willing to rectify or satisfy this issue, at least legally, thus they will not be able to collect income taxes from Citizens without enacting new laws. With the knowledge that all previous attempts to enact a Federal Individual Income Tax on the labor of Citizens of the 50 States have all been determined to be unconstitutional. This basically boxes them into a corner, a corner that would result in the admission by the U.S. Government, that they have been unlawfully collecting a Federal Individual Income Tax against Citizens of the 50 States since at WWII. It is their "Achilles Heel", if enough people are willing to challenge them and fight for the truth.

We will look at both material and circumstantial evidence to this effect. Much of which is the specific exhibits, Statutes and laws cut and pasted from the various government and legal websites that display them such as the country Records and Code of Federal Regulations and even the Internal Revenue Code itself, making it impossible for the information to be incorrect.

What you are going to observe and analyze in this book, if correct is amazing, if I have not missed any evidence that would nullify or invalidate my evidence and conclusions. That will however be up to you and others, as I have researched this well beyond the amount of time that I should have spent, and thus have decided to seek the consensus of the majority, for what I believe to be an extremely obvious conclusion. However, more heads are always better than one and I offer my evidence for you to weigh in on this injustice. I welcome your observations and evidence to help make my case.

The following is an example; a quote from a Court Case.

"In the event that the IRS files a defective Notice of Federal Tax Lien and the taxpayer is damaged, federal law also provides a remedy whereby the taxpayer can file a lawsuit in Federal District Court and be awarded damages if an IRS employee intentionally, recklessly or negligently disregarded the tax Code or any of its regulations with regard to collection activities." - IRC §7433. **(What Congress has giveth the Federal Courts can taketh away).** "Although §7433 gives a remedy for damages for the IRS's disregard of the Code and Regulations with regard to tax collection activities, the author has had personal experience with these lawsuits and opines that the Federal District Courts go out of their way to find reasons to dismiss these actions without affording the taxpayer the Congressionally mandated remedy)". - Andrew Clifton Moler - Tax Lawyer

From years of research, experience and discussions, there are many more Lawyers like Clifton Moler, that will affirm the above opinion, but few have the heart and fortitude to challenge the corrupt bureaucratic system and the Federal Judges that rubber stamp it, because retaliation against those that challenge their authority, has become an integral part of the confiscatory process.

When a person is treated as a criminal by our government for exposing criminal activity, we are then under the rule of criminals.

How do we restore justice and integrity back into our system? We have settled into a political and legal system strictly based on legalized force and coercion. Expecting it to be just, fair and full of people who support such justice and equality under the law is therefore a fool's errand. Attorneys indirectly or directly control all three branches of government and they are either too timid, to apathetic or to malevolent to alter the process for fear of losing their privilege, that of being a lawyer. The potential retaliatory nature of the system itself is also significant because it affords those practitioners the proverbial license to steal since they are the only ones allowed by their BAR Associations to earn money by representing other individuals and businesses in a Court of Law. If you have ever attempted to get a room full of attorneys to agree on anything, just go to a legislative session on an important topic at the State or Federal level. I don't foresee much hope under the current system. As politics has become, or perhaps always has been, an activity for the ambitious, catering to those special interests who are best afforded access to the public treasury. This seems to be the true nature of politics. The fact that our body politic has decriminalized perjury by politicians in their speech and by public prosecutors is an obvious result of the antithetic nature of government to the individual rights of the Citizens. How can a system work, where the rulers grant themselves legal protections, such as the protection from prosecution for perjury, or when a law exists to the contrary such as IRC §7433 noted above, where the Citizens have no realistic recourse?

People are basically only left with teaching one another and legally trying to fight the various abrogations and usurpations within the political system, hoping that it will one day spur change. Numerous government Prosecutors and Judges are themselves purposefully participating in thwarting justice. Part of their compensation is derived from the very taxes being assessed and enforced; an indisputable Conflict of Interest.

Of extreme importance, the Citizens, the various government employees, government Officials and the various Clerk(s) of Court around our Country must understand the significance of the issues presented and the attached Notification. The integrity and Rule of Law of our entire nation is at stake. We all read and see almost daily, the effects our dubious system of justice and the decaying Rule of Law are having on our Citizens and society. I therefore plead to everyone to take the time and energy to appraise themselves of the various issues addressed in this book and react accordingly; hopefully with truth and justice as your guide.

Dominant Issues At Large:

Are the Citizens of our nation going to continue to endure a "presumed" liability for a tax without some resemblance of "reasonable" redress and/or due process?

Does our body of law still protect Individual Property Rights, the Presumption of Innocence until proven guilty or liability is proven by an "impartial" court of law and

How do we insure impartial judicial decisions when the Judge's compensation/salaries are derived from the very taxes being levied and enforced when they are required by current decisions to pay Federal Individual Income Taxes because they are Officers of the Court?

What you are going to observe for yourself will be very disheartening once you have recognized and understood the ramifications. We have all heard, at some time in our lives, by crazy crackpots that there is no law that requires people to file and pay a Federal Individual Income Tax. That is wrong, but it is also correct. There are a very small minority of people who appear are required to file and pay a Federal Individual Income Tax. Most people, at least based on the laws I have researched for some 35 years, <u>are not</u> and are doing so under duress, fear, coercion, fraud and a system run amuck.

Form 668 (Y)(c)
(Rev. February 2004)

Department of the Treasury - Internal Revenue Service

Notice of Federal Tax Lien

Area: SMALL BUSINESS/SELF EMPLOYED AREA #3 Lien Unit Phone: (800) 913-6050	Serial Number	For Optional Use by Recording Office

As provided by section 6321, 6322, and 6323 of the Internal Revenue Code, we are giving a notice that taxes (including interest and penalties) have been assessed against the following-named taxpayer. We have made a demand for payment of this liability, but it remains unpaid. Therefore, there is a lien in favor of the United States on all property and rights to property belonging to this taxpayer for the amount of these taxes, and additional penalties, interest, and costs that may accrue.

CFN
OR BK RECORDED
Pala Beach County, Florida
Sharon R. Bock, CLERK & COMPTROLLER
Pg (1 pg)
PG

Name of Taxpayer

Residence

IMPORTANT RELEASE INFORMATION: For each assessment listed below, unless notice of the lien is refiled by the date given in column (e), this notice shall, on the day following such date, operate as a certificate of release as defined in IRC 6325(a).

Kind of Tax (a)	Tax Period Ending (b)	Identifying Number (c)	Date of Assessment (d)	Last Day for Refiling (e)	Unpaid Balance of Assessment (f)
1040	12/31/2009		12/17/2012	01/16/2023	1869.97
1040	12/31/2010		12/17/2012	01/16/2023	4653.02
1040	12/31/2011		12/24/2012	01/23/2023	4607.39

Place of Filing	County Courthouse Palm Beach County West Palm Beach, FL 33402	Total	$	11130.38

This notice was prepared and signed at _____BALTIMORE, MD_____, on this.

the ___06th___ day of ___March___, ___2013___.

Signature  for DEANN BENDER	Title ACS W&I (800) 829-7650	13-00-0000

(NOTE: Certificate of officer authorized by law to take acknowledgment is not essential to the validity of Notice of Federal Tax lien Rev. Rul. 71-466, 1971 - 2 C.B. 409)

Part 1 - Kept By Recording Office

Form **668(Y)(c)** (Rev. 2-2004)
CAT. NO 60025X

Book_____Page_____

Page 1 of 1

CHAPTER 2
MATERIAL EVIDENCE;
THE ERRONEOUS NFTL

On the previous page is a typical Notice of Federal Tax Lien (NFTL). After the assessment and notifications, the IRS sends the NFTL to the local Clerks of Court to be filed in the County Official Records where the taxpayer resides. It places an open Notice that there is a NFTL against all property of the individual or business named on the Lien. When these Liens are assessed by the IRS and presented to the Clerks of Court, they must be filed by Federal and State law and the Clerks of Court are protected by State Law and are not responsible in any way for their correctness, accuracy or legitimacy. We have notified, in writing, the local Clerks Office and this is what they had responded.

It is a purely a Federal Administrative Notice and Lien and therefore it does not require, under current practice, a court order, as required by;

Article V of the Bill of Rights; No person shall be....nor deprived of life, liberty or property, without due process of law.

You'll see later what kind of due process we are being afforded. If the government is assuming they are granting Due Process via their current system of Tax Courts, Collection Due Process (CDP) and other Equivalent Hearings, the Citizens of the Country, as you will see are being deceived by a "Kangaroo Court" system, as many other societies throughout history have experienced. A deception and an abomination of the rule of law as our Constitution was set out to protect. The entire system, especially at the Federal level is rigged by Judges and prosecutors who are willing to forgo the rule of law and Federal Statues to make sure the erroneous NFTL continues to be enforced.

Once the IRS has assessed an alleged liability against an individual or business and given them the various notices and time to review and challenge its accuracy, this Lien (NFTL) is sent out as their assessment. In Column (a) Kind of Tax, there is always a number which appears to relate to a Section in Title 26, Internal Revenue Code (IRC) or the Tax Form that denotes the so-called "Kind of Tax" you allegedly owe.

As you will see from the following NFTLs, there are numerous IRC Kinds of Tax Sections that are used on the various notices but none of them show the actual and correct Kind of Tax being levied. Is there any actual underlying Federal Statute that requires a Citizen from one of the 50 States to file and pay a Federal Individual Income Tax?

The numbers noted in column (a) "Kind of Tax" on the following NFTLs are the significant element of material evidence in this analysis and it does not require a rocket scientist to see their lack of legal standing.

As you will see the "Kind of Tax" the IRS has been assessing against most individuals and then issuing via the Notice of Federal Tax Lien (NFTL) they use for filing at the local County Courthouses is **incorrect** as to the Kind of Tax noted on the Notice of Federal Tax Lien. The IRS should, as required by a Federal Statute, (to be later examined more in depth), note the actual law that provides the Authority and Jurisdiction for the levy and enforcement of a Federal Individual Income Tax. "**They do not**", which makes them legally insufficient and therefore invalid to enforce.

This page has been intentionally left blank so the readers in "book" format can view the exhibit while they are reading the analysis at the same time.

Recording Requested By Internal Revenue
Service. When recorded mail to

INTERNAL REVENUE SERVICE
300 N Los Angeles St Mail Stop 5027
LOS ANGELES CA 90012

RECORDED/FILED IN OFFICIAL RECORDS
RECORDER'S OFFICE
LOS ANGELES COUNTY
CALIFORNIA

20090688224

May 11, 2009 AT 10:42 AM
FEE $12.00

For Optional Use by Recording Office

Form 668 (Y)(c) (Rev. October 2000)	Department of the Treasury - Internal Revenue Service **Notice of Federal Tax Lien**	

Area: SMALL BUSINESS/SELF EMPLOYED AREA #7
Lien Unit Phone: (800) 829-3903 — Serial Number

As provided by section 6321, 6322, and 6323 of the Internal Revenue Code, we are giving a notice that taxes (including interest and penalties) have been assessed against the following-named taxpayer. We have made a demand for payment of this liability, but it remains unpaid. Therefore, there is a lien in favor of the United States on all property and rights to property belonging to this taxpayer for the amount of these taxes, and additional penalties, interest, and costs that may accrue.

Name of Taxpayer ARNOLD SCHWARZENEGGER

Residence

IMPORTANT RELEASE INFORMATION: For each assessment listed below, unless notice of the lien is refiled by the date given in column (e), this notice shall, on the day following such date, operate as a certificate of release as defined in IRC 6325(a)

Kind of Tax (a)	Tax Period Ending (b)	Identifying Number (c)	Date of Assessment (d)	Last Day for Refiling (e)	Unpaid Balance of Assessment (f)
6721	12/31/2004	95-2980425	10/08/2007	11/07/2017	39047.20
6721	12/31/2005	95-2980425	08/04/2008	09/03/2018	40016.80

Place of Filing
COUNTY RECORDER
LOS ANGELES

Total $ 79064.00

This notice was prepared and signed at OAKLAND, CA , on this the 30 day of April 2009.

Signature R. A. Mitchell   Title TERRITORY MANAGER

(NOTE: Certificate of officer authorized by law to take acknowledgment is not essential to the validity of Notice of Federal Tax lien
Rev. Rul. 71-466, 1971-2 C.B. 409)

Part 1 - Kept By Recording Office

Form 668(Y)(c) (Rev. 10-00)
CAT. NO 60025X

On this NFTL, the "Kind of Tax" highlighted in gray tone in column (a) notes 6721. If you search:

Title 26, § 6721, it is titled: "Failure to file correct information returns."

This number, appears like others you will observe, to relate to a specific Section(s) denoted as (§) within Title 26 of the Internal Revenue Code.

While doing my research, I found this NFTL for Arnold Schwarzenegger, the actor and former Governor of California. You can search your County Official Records to see what NFTLs have been filed against individuals, as they are all public record. Additionally, there were various news reports showing the IRS filing a NFTL against Schwarzenegger.

This is a fairly common NFTL and can often be from an oversight by the individual. Arnold may have either forgotten to report some income from one of the many potential sources or perhaps had justifiable deductions that the IRS did not agree with. However his NFTL **does not show the underlying Kind or Type of Tax being levied**, but only an assessment for the failure to file a correct return, presumably meaning his Tax Return.

It is important to reiterate and understand that the "Kind of Tax" 6721, as do the others numbers that appear in this section of the NFTL, appear to represent "Sections"(§§) in Title 26 of the Internal Revenue Code (IRC) and even filing forms such as 1040 and 941, but do not provide the underlying Federal Statute, as is required.

Let's review. Is this a Kind of Tax or a penalty? Title 26, § 6721 is titled: Failure to file correct information returns.

What is the actual tax Schwarzenegger is allegedly supposed to be paying? What is the name of the actual legislative Act and when was this legislation passed? The following is from the

LA Times news article that appears to be a correct statement on the issues. LA Times of November 27, 2009 article Titled: **IRS files $79,000 tax lien against Schwarzenegger** – "The lien was reported this morning by TMZ.com, which posted a copy of a lien document that says it is from the county recorder's office. That document shows that Schwarzenegger owes $39,047.20 from 2004 and $40,016.80 from 2005. <u>The document also lists a section of the IRS Code that suggests the debt may be penalties for a failure to report certain business transactions.</u>"

As you can see, the NFTL does in fact appear to note that it is a penalty, as we have reviewed and not the Kind of Tax, as required by Federal Statute and thus should be insufficient as a lawful tax lien. Once again the Federal Statute will be examined later and the information that will be presented was copied by cutting and pasting it from the Statute itself to make sure every single word, phrase and punctuation mark was exactly as the Statute reads.

This obviously begs the question, what Kind of Tax did Schwarzenegger actually owe? As the NFTL does not specify the Kind or Type of Tax, but instead a penalty for failure to file a correct return.

So now let's see what some of the other elements noted on the NFTL are about and if they note any Kind or Type of Tax.

As you can see by looking at the previous NFTLs, the Sections within the IRC 6321, 6322 and 6323, are noted on them, above the Name of the Taxpayer. These IRC Sections have to do primarily with the authority to collect a tax. They "do not" note in them, any specific Federal Statute(s) that specifies the Kind of Tax being assessed, nor the jurisdiction(s) they are taxing as "actually" required by a real Federal Statute.

It does not appear that any of the other potential elements noted on the NFTL, provide us the specific Kind of Tax being assessed. Remember those IRC Section numbers, so we can go back to them later on in the book for more analysis. Right now, we want to continue to examine the issue of the Kind of Tax noted in column (a) on some other NFTLs. I just want to make it clear that the Kind of Tax noted in column (a) is the prominent issue of my contentious observations and conclusions. If anyone knows how to get in contact with Arnold, I would love to ask him if he has ever seen the actual Federal Statute that requires him to pay this alleged Federal Individual Income Tax. Not one single individual or entity I have ever asked or requested has been able to show me the Federal Statute and when it was passed. I always ask "when it was passed" so that there is no confusion as to the specific Act and when it was signed into law.

Form 668 (Y)(c)	Department of the Treasury - Internal Revenue Service
(Rev. February 2004)	**Notice of Federal Tax Lien**

Area: SMALL BUSINESS/SELF EMPLOYED AREA #3 Lien Unit Phone: (800) 913-6050	Serial Number	For Optional Use by Recording Office

As provided by section 6321, 6322, and 6323 of the Internal Revenue Code, we are giving a notice that taxes (including interest and penalties) have been assessed against the following-named taxpayer. We have made a demand for payment of this liability, but it remains unpaid. Therefore, there is a lien in favor of the United States on all property and rights to property belonging to this taxpayer for the amount of these taxes, and additional penalties, interest, and costs that may accrue.

Name of Taxpayer

Residence

IMPORTANT RELEASE INFORMATION: For each assessment listed below, unless notice of the lien is refiled by the date given in column (e), this notice shall, on the day following such date, operate as a certificate of release as defined in IRC 6325(a).

Kind of Tax (a)	Tax Period Ending (b)	Identifying Number (c)	Date of Assessment (d)	Last Day for Refiling (e)	Unpaid Balance of Assessment (f)
6672	03/31/2013		11/03/2014	12/03/2024	2690.40
6672	06/30/2013		11/03/2014	12/03/2024	16055.57
6672	09/30/2013		11/03/2014	12/03/2024	
6672	09/30/2013		04/13/2015	05/13/2025	42200.83
6672	12/31/2013		11/03/2014	12/03/2024	
6672	12/31/2013		04/13/2015	05/13/2025	32842.60
6672	03/31/2014		11/03/2014	12/03/2024	
6672	03/31/2014		04/13/2015	05/13/2025	38999.70

Place of Filing	County Courthouse Palm Beach County West Palm Beach, FL 33402	Total	$	132789.10

This notice was prepared and signed at _____ BALTIMORE, MD _____ . on this,

the __02nd__ day of __July__ , __2015__.

Signature _Cheryl Corderro_ for PATRICK M MOORE	Title REVENUE OFFICER (561) 616-2135	23-02-4543

(**NOTE:** Certificate of officer authorized by law to take acknowledgment is not essential to the validity of Notice of Federal Tax Lien Rev. Rul. 71-466, 1971 - 2 C.B. 409)

Part 1 - Kept By Recording Office

Form 668(Y)(c) (Rev. 2-2004)
CAT. NO 60025X

Book_____ Page_____   Page 1 of 1

On this NFTL, the "Kind of Tax" also appears to represent a <u>Section in Title 26</u> and in this case, Section 6672. Title 26, §6672 is titled:

"Failure to collect and pay over tax, or attempt to evade or defeat tax."

Interestingly enough, Section 6672 is under CHAPTER 68 titled, <u>ADDITIONS TO THE TAX, ADDITIONAL AMOUNTS, AND ASSESSABLE PENALTIES</u>, and Section 6672 is specifically under Subtitle B, PENALTIES. According to the Cornell University website, , Section 6672 "Authorities (CFR)"relates to 27 CFR, Titled: Alcohol, Tobacco Products and Firearms, 27 CFR Part 70 - PROCEDURE AND ADMINISTRATION - https://www.law.cornell.edu/uscode/text/26/6672 - This means the authority is derived from Title 27, Alcohol, Tobacco and Firearms and as such, is not "Positive Law". Perhaps it relates to those involved in products such as munitions and weapons, subject to Federal Authority? Generally for authority to be valid it comes from a legislative Act and describes the specific jurisdiction(s). Never the less, Section 6672 is a penalty and it does not designate as specific tax liability.

All the numbers shown under Kind of Tax, are three or four digit numbers, we must than try to ascertain what they represent. They appear to either relate to various Title 26 Sections or various Tax return filing forms. I am just assuming the number 6672 relates to a Penalty because of knowing the specific circumstances from other situations that I was privy to, having the same numbers on their NFTL. None of these other individuals were involved with anything to do with Alcohol, Tobacco or Firearms which this Section appears to gain its authority from.

Form 668 (Y)(c)
(Rev. February 2004)

Department of the Treasury - Internal Revenue Service

Notice of Federal Tax Lien

Area: SMALL BUSINESS/SELF EMPLOYED AREA #3 Lien Unit Phone: (800) 913-6050	Serial Number	For Optional Use by Recording Office

As provided by section 6321, 6322, and 6323 of the Internal Revenue Code, we are giving a notice that taxes (including interest and penalties) have been assessed against the following-named taxpayer. We have made a demand for payment of this liability, but it remains unpaid. Therefore, there is a lien in favor of the United States on all property and rights to property belonging to this taxpayer for the amount of these taxes, and additional penalties, interest, and costs that may accrue.

CFN OR BK
RECORDED
Sharon R. Bock, CLERK & COMPTROLLER
Palm Beach County, Florida
Pg (1 pg)
PG

Name of Taxpayer

Residence

IMPORTANT RELEASE INFORMATION: For each assessment listed below, unless notice of the lien is refiled by the date given in column (e), this notice shall, on the day following such date, operate as a certificate of release as defined in IRC 6325(a).

Kind of Tax (a)	Tax Period Ending (b)	Identifying Number (c)	Date of Assessment (d)	Last Day for Refiling (e)	Unpaid Balance of Assessment (f)
1040	12/31/2009		12/17/2012	01/16/2023	1869.97
1040	12/31/2010		12/17/2012	01/16/2023	4653.02
1040	12/31/2011		12/24/2012	01/23/2023	4607.39

Place of Filing	County Courthouse Palm Beach County West Palm Beach, FL 33402	Total	$	11130.38

This notice was prepared and signed at _____ BALTIMORE, MD _____ , on this,

the ___06th___ day of ___March___, ___2013___.

Signature for DEANN BENDER	Title ACS W&I (800) 829-7650	13-00-0000

(NOTE: Certificate of officer authorized by law to take acknowledgment is not essential to the validity of Notice of Federal Tax lien
Rev. Rul. 71-466, 1971 - 2 C.B. 409)

Part 1 - Kept By Recording Office

Form 668(Y)(c) (Rev. 2-2004)
CAT. NO 60025X

Book _____ Page _____

Page 1 of 1

On this NFTL, the *"Kind of Tax"* represents a Section in Title 26 is Section 1040. Title 26, §1040 is titled:

"Transfer of certain farm, etc., real property". (a) General rule If the executor of the estate of any decedent transfers to a qualified heir (within the meaning of section 2032A (e)(1)) any property with respect to which an election was made under section 2032A, then gain on such transfer shall be recognized to the estate only to the extent that, on the date of such transfer, the fair market value of such property exceeds the value of such property for purposes of chapter 11 (determined without regard to section 2032A).

The individual that received this NFTL, I have been conversing with, throughout their entire ordeal with the IRS. They did not receive any "estate" income, so how do we know if 1040 is a Section #, is this a number relating to the IRS Form 1040 or something else. FYI: The overwhelming majority of NFTLs researched have this number on them and it is highly unlikely that all the individuals researched had Estate Income as described in Title 26, §1040. It is therefore most likely relating to the 1040 tax form and there is no such thing as a 1040 Kind of Tax.

Are we supposed to just *assume* that there is some Federal Statute that requires us to pay an individual federal income tax because the NFTL surely doesn't tell us? Many others and I, as you will later see in this book, surely have never seen one and the government on every occasion of requesting it, has refused to provide the particular Federal Statute. Placing a 3 or 4 digit number that the lien holder must guess as to what Federal Statute it applies to, gives me pause, and leads me to my contention that these liens are invalid on their face. As you will see, the NFTL must show the *"Tax Liability Giving Rise To The Lien"*.

Form 668 (Y)(c) (Rev. February 2004)	Department of the Treasury - Internal Revenue Service **Notice of Federal Tax Lien**		

Area: SMALL BUSINESS/SELF EMPLOYED AREA #3 Lien Unit Phone: (800) 913-6050	Serial Number	For Optional Use by Recording Office

As provided by section 6321, 6322, and 6323 of the Internal Revenue Code, we are giving a notice that taxes (including interest and penalties) have been assessed against the following-named taxpayer. We have made a demand for payment of this liability, but it remains unpaid. Therefore, there is a lien in favor of the United States on all property and rights to property belonging to this taxpayer for the amount of these taxes, and additional penalties, interest, and costs that may accrue.

Name of Taxpayer

Residence

IMPORTANT RELEASE INFORMATION: For each assessment listed below, unless notice of the lien is refiled by the date given in column (e), this notice shall, on the day following such date, operate as a certificate of release as defined in IRC 6325(a).

Kind of Tax (a)	Tax Period Ending (b)	Identifying Number (c)	Date of Assessment (d)	Last Day for Refiling (e)	Unpaid Balance of Assessment (f)
1040	12/31/2005		11/17/2008	12/17/2018	8870.27
1040	12/31/2006		11/17/2008	12/17/2018	8639.64
6702	12/31/2000		08/04/2008	09/03/2018	5000.00
6702	12/31/2001		08/04/2008	09/03/2018	5000.00
6702	12/31/2002		08/04/2008	09/03/2018	5000.00
6702	12/31/2003		08/04/2008	09/03/2018	5000.00

Place of Filing
County Courthouse
Palm Beach County
West Palm Beach, FL 33402

Total $ 37509.91

This notice was prepared and signed at BALTIMORE, MD , on this,
the 17th day of December, 2009.

Signature R. A. Mitchell
for MS. K. KULANI

Title REVENUE OFFICER
(954) 423-7368
23-02-1810

(NOTE: Certificate of officer authorized by law to take acknowledgment is not essential to the validity of Notice of Federal Tax lien Rev. Rul. 71-466, 1971 - 2 C.B. 409)

Part 1 - Kept By Recording Office

Form 668(Y)(c) (Rev. 2-2004) CAT. NO 60025X

Book___/Page___   Page 1 of 1

With this NFTL, it was levied against another good friend. As you can see there are two numbers 1040 and 6702. We've discussed the 1040 and how it could be possibly based on one of two things. Either it denotes the filing form or and estate tax, neither of which note a correct and specific tax liability. A 1040 is a tax form and not a Kind of Tax and this individual had no estate income during those periods, so it is at the very least incorrect. Therefore, the IRS issued an erroneous "Notice of Federal Tax Lien" since the 1040 is incorrect.

So let's look at *§6702 titled:*

Frivolous Tax Submissions.

This individual was unwilling, actually unable to pay the tax, living near insolvency and having no Estate Income during the years in question.

They had filed a $0 Income Tax Return and thus were penalized and thus fined $5,000 for each of the three tax years in addition to the original assessment created by the original Substitute Return. They were not provided reasonable due process before this NFTL was filed. So to recap, not only did the IRS issue a NFTL under income that wasn't received by this individual, but they then penalized the individual for allegedly filing a frivolous income tax return. This is typical for the IRS to do this with little or no legal recourse. This author has personally experienced and has been privy to seeing these unjust filings against personal friends. As you will see later, they will ignore any question(s) relating to this issue. They have never answered what the number(s) mean in column (a) Kind of Tax.

Form 66B (Y)(c)	Department of the Treasury - Internal Revenue Service		
(Rev. February 2004)	**Notice of Federal Tax Lien**		

Area: SMALL BUSINESS/SELF EMPLOYED AREA #3 Lien Unit Phone: (800) 913-6050	Serial Number	For Optional Use by Recording Office

As provided by section 6321, 6322, and 6323 of the Internal Revenue Code, we are giving a notice that taxes (including interest and penalties) have been assessed against the following-named taxpayer. We have made a demand for payment of this liability, but it remains unpaid. Therefore, there is a lien in favor of the United States on all property and rights to property belonging to this taxpayer for the amount of these taxes, and additional penalties, interest, and costs that may accrue.

CFN
OR BK PG
RECORDED 09:41:22
Palm Beach County, Florida
Sharon R. Bock, CLERK & COMPTROLLER
Pg (1 pg)

Name of Taxpayer █████████

Residence ████████████

IMPORTANT RELEASE INFORMATION: For each assessment listed below, unless notice of the lien is refiled by the date given in column (e), this notice shall, on the day following such date, operate as a certificate of release as defined in IRC 6325(a).

Kind of Tax (a)	Tax Period Ending (b)	Identifying Number (c)	Date of Assessment (d)	Last Day for Refiling (e)	Unpaid Balance of Assessment (f)
1120	12/31/2012	████	09/23/2013	10/23/2023	3507.92
6721	12/31/2010	████	12/02/2013	01/01/2024	
6721	12/31/2010	████	12/09/2013	01/08/2024	1625.27
941	12/31/2012	████	09/02/2013	10/02/2023	281.61

Place of Filing	County Courthouse Palm Beach County West Palm Beach, FL 33402	Total	$	5414.80

This notice was prepared and signed at _____BALTIMORE, MD_____ , on this,

the ___24th___ day of ___February___ ___2014___.

Signature for PATRICK M MOORE	Title REVENUE OFFICER (561) 616-2135	23-02-4543

(**NOTE:** Certificate of officer authorized by law to take acknowledgment is not essential to the validity of Notice of Federal Tax Lien Rev. Rul. 71-466, 1971 - 2 C.B. 409)

Part 1 - Kept By Recording Office

Form **668(Y)(c)** (Rev. 2-2004)
CAT. NO 60025X

Book ████ /Page ████

Page 1 of 1

Let's look at just one more NFTL with three different numbers on it as the Kind of Tax.

Highlighted in gray tone are the Kind of Tax in column (a) for this NFTL. Three numbers 1120, 6721 and 941 are noted as a Kind of Tax. 6721 is the same number as we saw with Arnold Schwarzenegger's NFTL, a penalty and not an actual Kind of Tax.

I then looked up the United States Code, Title 26, §1120, and low and behold there is no such section in the IRC or the United States Code. It probably then must be an IRS filing form because when I looked it up the only reference I found to anything relating to taxes was the number IRS Form# 1120, a **U.S. Corporation Income Tax Return**. The named party on this NFTL just happens to be a business and a corporation.

Once again, obviously an IRS income tax form number does not specify a Kind of Tax. It's a tax form and as we saw before with the 1040 number, it could represent a section under Title 26 but it does not. We however really don't know for sure, except that 1040 is a Federal Individual Income Tax form and 1120 is the U.S. Corporate Income tax form and they are two of the most common numbers noted, along with 940 and 941 on the various NFTLs I researched.

The last number 941 that is noted on this NFTL is a Section of the IRC that has been repealed and like both 1040 and 1120, 941 is also a form number.

This is cut and pasted directly from the 26 USC:
26 USC Sec. 941
TITLE 26 - INTERNAL REVENUE CODE
Subtitle A - Income Taxes
CHAPTER 1 - NORMAL TAXES AND SURTAXES
Subchapter N - Tax Based on Income From Sources Within or Without the United States

PART III - INCOME FROM SOURCES WITHOUT THE UNITED STATES
[Subpart E - Repealed]
[Sec. 941. Repealed. Pub. L. 108-357, title I, Sec. 101(b)(1), Oct. 22, 2004, 118 Stat. 1423] Section, added Pub. L. 106-519, Sec. 3(b), Nov. 15, 2000, 114 Stat. 2424, related to qualifying foreign trade income.

Form 941 relates to the Form an Employer is supposed to file when they collect income taxes from the employees and then must pay that money to the IRS quarterly. Supporting the probability that 941, as with 1120 are filing forms and in both instances the Named Taxpayer were business corporations. After reviewing this form, as with the previous ones such as the1040 and 1120, there is no notation or declaration on the form itself or the instructions as to the specific Kind of Tax being imposed. Why would they not put the Federal Statute that provides them the authority and jurisdiction on the NFTL?

In the Instructions relating to Tax Form 941, it states that "Section 6011 requires you to provide the requested information if the tax is applicable to you", but it does not tell us if the section, Titled Chapter 61 – INFORMATION AND RETURNS is applicable to any specific jurisdictions, nor does it state a specific Federal Statute granting it's authority for the underlying Kind or Type of Tax. This is what we are trying to identify.

You would assume that the form itself would also have something to the extent of;

"As required by Section _____ Title _____United States Code _____ the above named individual/business, a Taxpayer is hereby liable for the unpaid balance of the Assessment noted in column

_____ "......so that the NFTL could then be legally sufficient as a Tax Lien., but they do not.

Even if some sort of Federal Statute is found in the instructions or some other place on one of the various forms, it does not qualify the NFTL as being perfected as a valid Lien. As you will see, the NFTL must note the "Tax Liability Giving Rise To The Lien" and not some three or four digit number that we are not sure what it represents or what it even means. That and other evidence will be provided later.

What really spurred my initial interest in this issue was the lack of transparency and the extremely puzzling observations that the IRS appeared to make a concerted effort "not" to place the underlying Federal Regulation on any of the forms, correspondence and liens. It wasn't until I more closely reviewed the actual Form 1040, because none of the other forms or the NFTL itself had it on them, that I was even able to verify the alleged name of the Tax; "Federal Individual Income Tax." Only one other form, letter or lien that has been sent to me and others that I've reviewed has had any name of a kind or type of tax on it, and it just noted "Personal Income" and not even the word tax after it. That form letter is also an exhibit later on in the book.

When I mean by none of the other forms, letters or liens, I'm including about 8 to 12 different documents. So let's continue looking at just a couple more NFTLs that I found in my research.

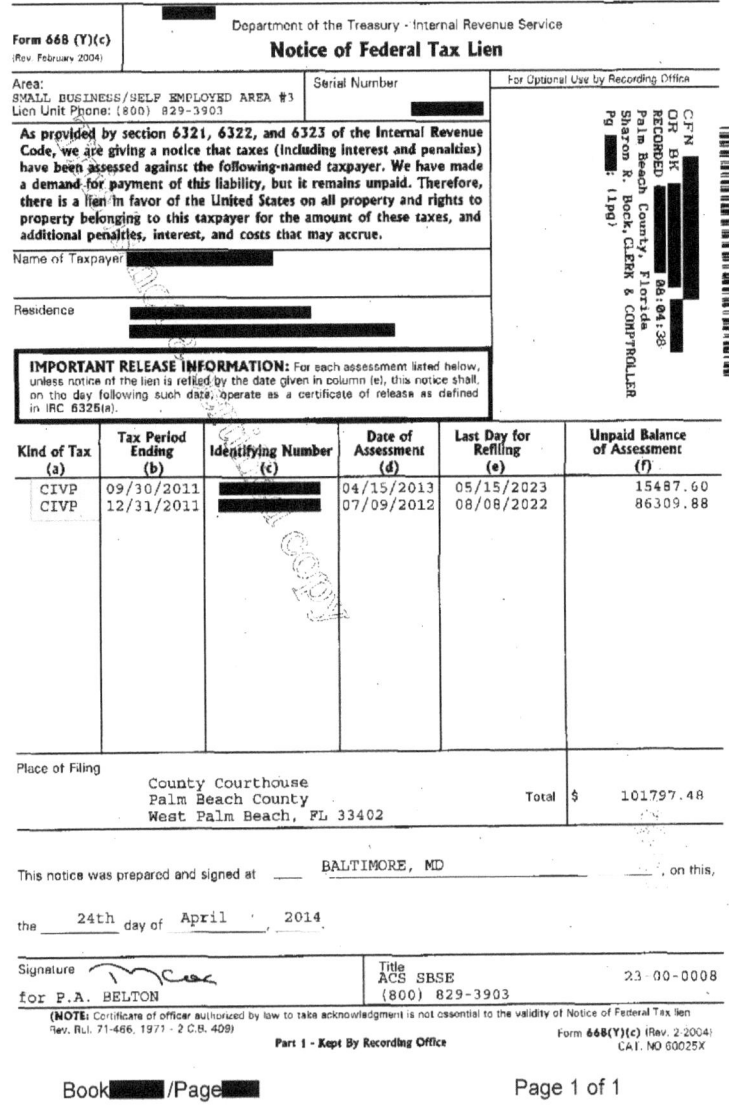

In this case the "Kind of Tax" is noted as Civil (CIV.) and Proceedings (P). or (CIVP). So what Kind of Tax is the individual paying in this case? Who the heck knows and I'm sure the alleged taxpayer has had a wonderful time going through this process and hopefully they were represented by a good attorney!

I researched this particular NFTL to find out how one would get the CIVP as the Kind of Tax on their NFTL. I can only assume the individual went to what is the Federal Tax Court which is composed of nineteen (19) Presidential appointees and thus the final Assessment was determined by some sort of Judicial Proceedings. This is the group of people most of us don't even know exist but they have a very nice website.

Once again, what Kind of Tax is being imposed? It reminds me of that old cliché I first heard as a kid. "It's for me to know and for you to find out".

Summary of Material Evidence

<u>Of the 200+ NFTL's researched, a vast majority of the liens noted 1040 and 941 under the Kind of Tax in column (a).</u>

We've seen that 1040 could either be an Estate Tax but most likely just the number for the 1040 Form. Neither of the two individuals whose situations I was privy to, had estate income thus their Liens are incorrect because obviously a 1040 Form is not a Kind of Tax. With so many people receiving NFTLs noting the number 1040 on them, it is highly improbable most of them had Estate Income, thus the majority of them are also incorrect.

It appears the IRS has been issuing, over the years, hundreds of thousands, if not millions of erroneous "Notice of Federal Tax Liens" (NTFL) against Americans using various erroneous Kinds of Tax and this would "suggest" a potential ongoing fraud against the Citizens of the Country. Let us continue on our journey to find the truth in these matters before us.

From my research, the 941 Kind of Tax is the second most prominent Kind of Tax type filed by the IRS on NFTLs.

As previously shown Title 26 U.S. Code § 941 to 943 is titled: Repealed. Section 941, added Pub. L. 106–519, § 3(b), Nov. 15, 2000, 114 Stat. 2424 but relates to qualifying foreign trade income.

Since most individuals do not have foreign trade income, just like with the 1040, the IRS appears to be using the IRS Tax Form 941 on the Notice of Federal Tax Liens being issued against thousands or even hundreds of thousands of businesses.

Why don't they correctly note the Federal Statute for the underlying tax on the Liens instead of a tax form number? Even the various penalties only show the Section within Title 26 relating to the Penalty and not the underlying Tax liability for which the penalty is being assessed under.

The reason why? We can only assume the reason the IRS does not show the correct authority designations for the Kind of Federal Individual Income Tax is, as you will come see for yourself, is that there does not appear to be a Federal Statute that has ever been enacted that would require most Citizens of the 50 States, as individuals working in a private capacity to file and pay a Federal Individual Income Tax on their individual labor. However, that issue is really moot for this evaluation, because the NFTL appears to note erroneous Kinds of Tax on them and thus they are invalid anyway. The Government cannot or <u>should not</u> be able to "legally" collect on an invalid Notice of Federal Tax Lien but they do every day.

Although it is logical to conclude that if a government agency, or anyone for that matter, files a lien against somebody else, that it must correctly note the legal authority (law) and/or the

"Kind of Tax" on the lien itself. In this case, it should be a United States Statute that qualifies as "positive law" or a Statue within the Code of Federal Statutes, referring to a specific enactment(s) passed by Congress at some time in our history that would thus become a part of Title 26, Internal Revenue Code and published as such.

I have shown just a few of the three or four digit numbers shown in column (a) Kinds of Tax the IRS uses on their NFTLs, but they use many others. They all however, appear to be just like the ones already exhibited, in that they are either tax forms or they appear to represent various Sections within the IRC, and thusly would provide no additional relevant information to our discussion. I welcome you to look up additional Notices of Federal Tax Liens to verify what I have presented to you. http://www.mypalm-beachclerk.com/officialrecords/search.aspx

I do show some more numbers for the alleged Kind of Taxes later in the book but also I found various numbers on the NFTLs I researched. Those that I found, all appear to relate to either a section of the IRC or a tax return form, except for the one I believe relates to Civil Proceedings (CIVP).

The problem with these numbers is that I could never positively identify what these numbers stood for and only by association, was I ever able to place a number to a specific Section or Form. Never clearly being sure of my conclusion, which could of course be alleviated by the IRS simply placing the specific Federal Statute on their various forms, and thus their lawful authority and jurisdiction(s) being taxed. You will see later why the IRS probably does not and will not do this.

CHAPTER 3
EVIDENCE OF REQUIRED ELEMENTS (NFTL)

To make absolutely sure what elemental or content disclosures, specifically the "Kind of Tax" on the NFTL that is required for it to be legally sufficient, we must look to the various laws and regulations regarding the requirements that the Treasury and IRS must disclose on the Notice of Federal Tax Lien for it to be a valid lien.

Does the correct Kind of Tax, as designated by a specific Federal Statute have to be disclosed, noted on the NFTL, for it to be a legal disclosure and a valid lien against a Citizen? Obviously, you would think so.

I believe it becomes a question of due process. Has the IRS, through the issuance of the NFTL, <u>properly informed and disclosed</u> to the Citizen that they owe a specific tax because of a specific enacted Federal Statute? If so, then the Citizen might utilize that law to determine if there is a potential liability and how much that liability would be under that law. I believe this is a fair question to ask and see if we can ascertain the answer.

U.S. law is organized as the United States Code. Income, estate, gift, and excise tax provisions, plus provisions relating to tax returns and enforcement, were codified as Title 26. It is generally labeled as United States Code Title 26 Section(s) (§§) _____,**and are general statutes of a permanent nature currently in force for a <u>specific jurisdiction.</u>** (from Wikipedia.) http://www.loc.gov/law/help/statutes.php - (Library of Congress.)

Statutes are laws (or Acts) passed by the Legislature and signed by the President. As you know, these legislative acts can become law with or without the approval of the President under various circumstances, such as overriding a veto. Federal statutes

may be published in two formats: public and private laws and codified law. Public and private laws are published in the format that
are usually signed by the two chambers of the United States Congress and the President. Codified law is published in a subject ar-
ranged format. Codes are commonly called current law because a
code section consists of the original law that created the code section and subsequent amendments integrated together. Both public
and private laws and codified law are available in print and elec-
tronic form. Statutes may be found by using the citation, the pop-
ular name, or by subject. The current edition of the United States
Code was published in 2012, and according to the Government
Printing Office, is over 200,000 pages long.

Statutes are published in chronological order by date of
passage. Most citations consist of the public law number and its
location in the *United States Statutes at Large* (Example: Pub. L.
108-45, 107 Stat. 25). Each law receives a unique public or private
law number which has two parts: the number of the U. S. Congress, and a sequentially assigned number (Example: Pub. L. 108-
45 is the 45th law passed during the 108th Congress). The location
of this public law is in *United States Statutes at Large*, volume
107 page 25.

Subject Arrangement of Statutes:

A code, such as the Internal Revenue Code is a subject arrangement of general statutes of a permanent nature currently in force for a specific jurisdiction. Laws passed by the U. S. Congress have been compiled into two codes: *Revised Statutes of 1875* and the *United States Code*, which began in 1926. The *Revised Statutes of 1875* is a compilation of statutes enacted during the period of 1789 through 1873. It is only necessary to consult the *Revised Statutes of 1875,* if a statute was repealed after the compilation of the *Revised Statutes* but prior to the first compilation of the *United States Code*. A copy of the *Revised Statutes* is located at the **Reference Desk** and **Row 5.**

So when you receive a NTFL, how does one know which of the various taxes a Citizen is being assessed? How would one know which Federal Statute it would specifically apply to, what specific jurisdiction it applies to and when it was passed? As you can see, our system of laws does not make it easy to determine this.

The **authority** for the material in the United States Code comes from its enactment through the legislative process and not from its presentation in the Code. For example, the United States Code omitted 12 U.S.C. § 92 for decades, apparently because it was thought to have been repealed. In its 1993 ruling in *U.S. National Bank of Oregon v. Independent Insurance Agents of America*, 508 U.S. 439, 440 (1993), the Supreme Court ruled that §92 was still a valid law.

In United States v. Zuger, 602 F. Supp. 889, 891 (D. Conn. 1984) ("Where a title has, however, been enacted into positive law, the Code title itself is deemed to constitute conclusive evidence of the law; recourse to other sources is unnecessary and precluded.")

So we have established by the two appellate cases above, a few things. **1. Authority does not come from the Code itself, but from the enactment of a Federal Statute and 2. That it must be Positive Law for it to be conclusive evidence of the law. Just because it is a Code, does not mean that it is positive law and that will be addressed later in the book.**

These two issues are however, only circumstantial evidence in support of the material evidence that has been previously provided in relation to the erroneous "Kind(s) of Tax" being noted on the NFTL by the IRS. We still need to conclusively determine by law, if the NFTLs are invalid, because of the lack of a correct notation on the NFTL of the "Kind of Tax" being levied and enforced.

We will go back, address and provide the necessary information on these issues later, but we want to continue to focus on trying to determine if the NFTL's are legally sufficient as valid liens, since they appear to never show the correct Kind of Tax on them.

From the IRS Manual;

Internal Revenue Manual
5.17.2 Federal Tax Liens
Part 5. Collecting
Chapter 17. Legal Reference Guide for Revenue Officers Section 2. Federal Tax Liens5.17.2.3.4 (03-27-2012) Contents of Notice of Federal Tax Lien "The Secretary of Treasury prescribes the form and content of the NFTL" and the NFTL is valid notwithstanding any other provisions of law regarding the form or content. IRC § 6323(f) (3). "The NFTL can be either a paper form (the Service uses Form 668(Y)), or a form transmitted electronically, including by fax or e-mail. Regardless of the method used to file the

NFTL, it must identify the taxpayer, THE TAX LIABILITY GIVING RISE TO THE LIEN, and the date the assessment arose. - Treas. Reg. § 301.6323(f)-1(d) (2)."

As we assumed, based on law and common sense, it appears very clear that the Treasury Secretary prescribes the content of the NFTL, that the NFTL must note **THE TAX LIABILITY GIVING RISE TO THE LIEN**, as per the Internal Revenue Manual and, **the character of the liability assessed** as per Title 26 CFR 301.6203-1 –

In Sills v. United States 82 F.3d 111. The Court acknowledges:

Section 6323 of the Internal Revenue Code states that a lien shall not be valid "as against any purchaser, holder of a security interest, mechanic's lienor, or judgment lien creditor until notice thereof which meets the requirements of subsection (f) has been filed by the Secretary." I.R.C. § 6323(a) (1994). Subsection (f) provides, inter alia, that "[t]he form and content of the notice ... shall be prescribed by the Secretary." I.R.C. § 6323(f) (1994). The applicable IRS regulation requires that the lien specify: (1) the taxpayer, (2) the tax liability giving rise to the lien, and (3) the date that the assessment arose. 26 C.F.R. § 301.6323(f)-1(d)(2) (1995). Additionally: Treasury Reg. 301.6323(f)-1(d) further provides that: "the notice of federal tax lien must be filed on a Form 668, Notice of Federal Tax Lien under Internal Revenue Laws, and must identify the taxpayer, the tax liability giving rise to the lien, and the date the assessment arose".

Obviously, from Federal Regulations, the IRC, Treasury Regulations, Appellate Case Laws and the IRS Manual itself, they all support the conclusion that the content of the NFTL must note **"the tax liability giving rise to the lien"**. Therefore there must have been a Federal Statue passed and that Statute or its Codified

Title and Section must be noted on the form. However, as you have seen on the various Notice of Federal Tax Liens and various other forms, they do not correctly note any Statutes and instead note a three or four digit number that only appears to relate to either a Section of the IRC or other Title, a penalty within the IRC or an IRS Form, with no indication of which one it is.

Additionally, as I noted earlier on an NFTL there are generally three IRC Code Sections noted, 6321, 6322 and 6323. They note:

"Title 26 U.S.C. Sec. 6323(f) (3) Form" *The form and content of the notice referred to in subsection (a) shall be prescribed by the Secretary. Such notice shall be valid notwithstanding any other provision of law regarding the form or content of a notice of lien. Sub Section (a) of Sec. 6323, Purchasers, holders of security interests, mechanic's lienors, and judgment lien creditors. The lien imposed by section 6321 shall not be valid as against any purchaser, holder of a security interest, mechanic's lienor, or judgment lien creditor until notice thereof which meets the requirements of subsection (f) has been filed by the Secretary.*

26 U.S.C. Sec. 6321 *- If any person liable to pay any tax neglects or refuses to pay the same after demand, the amount (including any interest, additional amount, addition to tax, or assessable penalty, together with any costs that may accrue in addition thereto) shall be a lien in favor of the United States upon all property and rights to property, whether real or personal, belonging to such person.*

26 U.S.C. Sec. 6321(f) Place for filing notice; form." *"26 CFR 301.6203-1 - Method of assessment.* *The district director and the director of the regional service center shall appoint one or more assessment officers. The district director shall also appoint assessment officers in a Service Center servicing his district. The assessment shall*

*be made by an assessment officer signing the summary rec-
ord of assessment. The summary record, through supporting records, shall provide identification of the taxpayer, **the
character of the liability assessed**, the taxable period, if applicable, and the amount of the assessment. The amount of
the assessment shall, in the case of tax shown on a return
by the taxpayer, be the amount so shown, and in all other
cases the amount of the assessment shall be the amount
shown on the supporting list or record. The date of the assessment is the date the summary record is signed by an
assessment officer. If the taxpayer requests a copy of the
record of assessment, he shall be furnished a copy of the
pertinent parts of the assessment which set forth the name
of the taxpayer, the date of assessment, **the character of the
liability assessed**, the taxable period, if applicable, and the
amounts assessed. "*

These were cut and pasted from the IRC and they do not
directly relate to a specific "Tax Liability Giving Rise to the Lien"
but only provide some operational and regulatory provisions under Chapter 64 Collections.

Additionally, the Individual's Master File (IMF) or Business Master File (BMF) transcript of a taxpayer's account is supposed to contain all of the information required under Treas. Reg.
§ 301.6203-1.

Internal Revenue Code section 6203 states:
**an "assessment shall be made by recording the liability of
the taxpayer in the office of the Secretary** in accordance
with rules or regulations prescribed by the Secretary. Upon
request of the taxpayer, the Secretary shall furnish the taxpayer a copy of the record of the assessment. " Thus, a federal determination is final on the date on which the adjust-*

ment resulting from an Internal Revenue Service examination is assessed. (Rev. & Tax. Code section 18622, subdivision (d); Internal Revenue Code section 6203.)"

Requirements for lawful, procedurally proper assessments are prescribed by 26 CFR § 301.6203-1. In order for there to be a lawful, procedurally proper assessment, the assessment certificate must positively identify the taxpayer, **the class or kind of tax,** the amount, and the date of assessment. The date of assessment is the date on which an assessment officer signs the assessment certificate.

Both 26 U.S.C. § 6203 and the regulation assures taxpayers of the right to secure copies of assessment certificates on request. There is no tax liability until the tax is assessed.

"For approximately three years there has been a coordinated effort to secure copies of assessment certificates but it appears that Internal Revenue Service assessment officers haven't executed lawful, procedurally proper income tax assessment certificates for two decades or longer." The Parallel Table of Authorities and Rules does not list 26 CFR Part 1 or 31 authority for 26 U.S.C. § 6203 so it does not appear that the IRS has authority to assess income taxes." – from **The Family Guardian.**

One of the individuals for whom I personally know, requested his Individual Master File. Upon examination of the IMF, he was shown as being engaged in the sale of off road diesel and jet fuel, which of course he was not. He was a welder/fabricator. He never was able to obtain a corrected IMF noting his correct occupation. Perhaps those involved in the sale of off road diesel and jet fuel are required to pay this taxes?

Various "Kinds of Tax"

Kind of Tax	U.S. Statute	Title	Category	Form
Unk	Title 26 §1	Tax imposed	Income Tax	1040
Unk	Title 26 §6414	Income Tax Withheld	Income Tax	941
1040	Title 26 §1040	Transfer of certain farm, etc., real property	Estate	706
6721	Title 26 §6721	Failure to file correct information returns	Penalty	N/A
941	Title 26 §941	Qualifying foreign trade income	Foreign Trade Inc	8873
6702	Title 26 §6702	Frivolous Tax Submissions	Penalty	N/A
6672	Title 26 §6672	Failure to collect and pay over tax, or attempt to evade or defeat tax	Penalty	N/A
6722	Title 26 § 6722	Failure to furnish correct payee statements	Penalty	N/A
*CIVP	26 USC § 7403	Action to enforce lien on subject property to payment of tax	Civil Proceedings	N/A

The above chart is a spread sheet I put together of some of the research conducted to make it easier to review the previous pages as to the "Kind of Tax" most often appearing to be related to either various Section(s) (§§) within Title 26 or an IRS Tax Form.

As previously stated, from researching public records of NFTLs filed by the IRS against hundreds of people, the IRS appears to be assessing most individuals with the Kind of Tax, a "1040" being noted on the Notice of Federal Tax Liens. What "Kind of Tax" is it really supposed to be since most people interviewed did not have any Estate Income?

Again, **why don't they utilize the actual Congressional Act and when it was passed?** As you will be shown, no one from any Agency of the Government, the Judiciary or Congress themselves, have been able or willing to answer this question or provide the Federal Statue a "1040 Kind of Tax" relates to.

Other Kind of Tax Types and Subtypes

http://www.fms.treas.gov/eftps/marketing/fr_ets_same_day.pdf e_day.pdf

Form Number	Form Name	Tax Type Prefix (First 4 Digits)	Valid Suffixes (Last Digit—see Legend below)	Valid Months
		Common IRS Tax Types and Subtypes		
720	Quarterly Excise Tax	7200	3, 4, 5, 7, 8, 9, B	03, 06, 09, 12
940	Employer's Annual Unemployment Tax	0940	3, 4, 5, 7, 8, 9, B	12
941	Employer's Quarterly Tax	9410	0, 3, 4, 5, 7, 8, 9, B	03, 06, 09, 12
944	Employer's Annual Federal Tax	9440	0, 1, 3, 4, 5, 7, 8, 9, B	12
945	Withheld Federal Income Tax	0945	0, 3, 4, 5, 7, 8, 9, B	12
990T	Exempt Organization Business Income Tax	9904	2, 3, 4, 6, 7, 8, 9, B	Fiscal Year Month (01-12)
1042	Annual Withholding Tax for U.S. Source Income of Foreign Persons	1042	2, 3, 4, 6, 7, 8, 9, B	12
1120	Corporation Income Tax Federal	1120	0, 2, 3, 4, 6, 7, 8, 9, B	Fiscal Year Month (01-12)
2290	Heavy Vehicle Use Tax	2290	3, 4, 7, 8, 9, B	01-12
8804	Annual Return of Partnership Withholding Tax (Section 1446)	8804	3, 4, 7, 8, 9, B	01-12

Legend for Tax Type Suffixes (the one character suffix follows the 4-digit prefix number):

Suffix	Type	Suffix	Type
0	Amended	6	Estimated
2	Extension	7	Subsequent/With Return
3	Designated Pymt of Fees or Collection Costs	8	Designated Payment of Interest
4	Advanced Payment of Determined Deficiency	9	Designated Payment of Penalty
5	Payment	B	IRS 6603 Deposits (cash bond)

An extensive search was done on the "Kind of Tax" under Title 26 and related laws and as you can see from this government document, nothing specific from the IRS or Treasury Department supplies any relevant information. The most common 1040 tax form is not even noted on this chart and the Tax Type Prefixes relate to the Form Number and not the section under Title 26, Internal Revenue Code or the Code of Federal Regulations.

 **IRS** Department of the Treasury
Internal Revenue Service
CCP-LU ACS
P.O. BOX 24017, STOP 76101
FRESNO, CA 93779-4017

CERTIFIED MAIL

7105 5678 7185 0304 4409

(EXHIBIT A)
2 OF 5

Letter Date: 10/11/2011
Taxpayer Identification Number:
XXX-XX-████
Person to Contact:
PAMELA J ROGERS
Contact Telephone Number:
(800) 829-7650
Employee Identification Number:
████████

100568

Notice of Federal Tax Lien Filing and Your Right to a Hearing Under IRC 6320

Dear ████████████:

We filed a Notice of Federal Tax Lien on 10/13/2011 .

Type of Tax	Tax Period	Assessment Date	Amount on Lien
1040	12/31/2005	02/14/2011	7327.16
1040	12/31/2006	02/14/2011	4497.07
1040	12/31/2009	12/13/2010	12747.51

NOTE: Please contact the person whose name and telephone number appears on this notice to obtain the current amount you owe. Additional interest and penalties may be increasing the amount on the lien shown above.

A lien attaches to all property you currently own and to all property you may acquire in the future. It also may damage your credit rating and hinder your ability to obtain additional credit.

You have the right to a hearing with us to appeal this collection action and to discuss your payment method options. To explain the different collection appeal procedures available to you, we have enclosed Publication 1660, Collection Appeal Rights.

You must request your hearing by 11/21/2011 . Please complete the enclosed Form 12153, *Request for a Collection Due Process or Equivalent Hearing,*and mail it to:

Internal Revenue Service
IRS-ACS/CDP
P.O. BOX 24017, STOP 76180
FRESNO, CA 93779-4017

Letter 3172 (DO) rev. (2-2008)
Catalog No. 297871

This is one of the many IRS Form Letters provided as additional evidence to help determine if the IRS is improperly noticing individuals and not specifically noting the correct "Kind of Tax" being imposed. On this page and the next three pages, you will see some additional evidence of this.

This is the Notice from the IRS informing the individual that a NFTL has been filed against them and their rights to a Collection Due Process (CDP) Hearing.

As you can see on this letter they are calling it a "**Type of Tax**", with 1040 noted as the type. What we now know it is not an Estate Tax under Section 1040 and it is most likely the tax form. This is the individual I wrote about previously that had not received any Estate income during the periods noted.

As you will read later, prior to any hearing, under Title 5, of the Administrative Procedures Act (APA) the IRS is required to provide their Authority, thus enabling them to be doing what they are doing. That of assessing and collecting the Federal Individual Income Tax. When we requested their authority, they just ignored us, even though we did it in writing. They then denied the request for the hearing based on the grounds you will read later.

Why they denote a *Type of Tax* on this form as compared to a Kind of Tax on the NFTLs is unknown to me at this time.

Form **12153** (Rev. 12-2013)	**Request for a Collection Due Process or Equivalent Hearing**

Use this form to request a Collection Due Process (CDP) or equivalent hearing with the IRS Office of Appeals if you have been issued one of the following lien or levy notices:

- Notice of Federal Tax Lien Filing and Your Right to a Hearing under IRC 6320,
- Notice of Intent to Levy and Notice of Your Right to a Hearing,
- Notice of Jeopardy Levy and Right of Appeal,
- Notice of Levy on Your State Tax Refund,
- Notice of Levy and Notice of Your Right to a Hearing.

Complete this form and send it to the address shown on your lien or levy notice. Include a copy of your lien or levy notice to ensure proper handling of your request.

Call the phone number on the notice or 1-800-829-1040 if you are not sure about the correct address or if you want to fax your request.

You can find a section explaining the deadline for requesting a Collection Due Process hearing in this form's instructions. If you've missed the deadline for requesting a CDP hearing, you must check line 7 (Equivalent Hearing) to request an equivalent hearing.

1. Taxpayer Name: (Taxpayer 1) _____

   Taxpayer Identification Number _____

   Current Address _____

   City _____ State _____ Zip Code _____

2. Telephone Number and Best Time to Call During Normal Business Hours

   Home (___) ___ - _____ ☐ am. ☐ pm.
   Work (___) ___ - _____ ☐ am. ☐ pm.
   Cell (___) ___ - _____ ☐ am. ☐ pm.

3. Taxpayer Name: (Taxpayer 2) _____

   Taxpayer Identification Number _____

   Current Address _____
   (If Different from Address Above) City _____ State _____ Zip Code _____

4. Telephone Number and Best Time to Call During Normal Business Hours

   Home (___) ___ - _____ ☐ am. ☐ pm.
   Work (___) ___ - _____ ☐ am. ☐ pm.
   Cell (___) ___ - _____ ☐ am. ☐ pm.

5. Tax Information as Shown on the Lien or Levy Notice *(If possible, attach a copy of the notice)*

(1) Type of Tax (Income, Employment, Excise, etc. or Civil Penalty)	(2) Tax Form Number (1040, 941, 720, etc)	Tax Period or Periods

As you can see this is Form 12153 "Request for a Collection Due Process or Equivalent Hearing" commonly referred to as a CDP hearing. The CDP was attached to the 3172 Form letter discussed on the prior two pages. On the bottom left hand side of the page, the gray tone highlight, the form notes Type of Tax on the top of the 1st Column and Tax Form Number on the top of the 2nd column.

This was interesting to me because this is a form that the individual must fill out themselves if they want to request a CDP hearing. The IRS does not note the Kind of Tax, but wants the taxpayer to fill the information in. In law this is what would be called admission of guilt. We now know that we really don't know the Type of Tax we are supposed to be paying because it is never noted on any of the forms being presented except on forms we are allegedly supposed to fill out like the 1040 form. What "type" or "Kind" of tax would you write in this box now that you at least know something about this issue?

When my good friend filed this form after I showed her the evidence, she put unknown under both columns because she really didn't know. Of course, as you will see later, she was denied a CDP hearing. She had requested the IRS/Treasury authority and jurisdiction and the actual statutory requirement for the administrative agency with taxing powers. Apparently they didn't like that.

Even though, the IRS never put the correct Type or Kind of Tax being imposed on any of their forms or correspondence, this form shows the Type of Tax is different from the Tax Form number and that 1040 is one of the acknowledged Tax Forms, being enforced. The IRS, at this point, already knows what Kind of Tax you "reportedly" owe, as they have already assessed and filed a NFTL against the named Taxpayer. Not putting the Kind of Tax you allegedly owe on this form is just another example of the kind of games they play to get people to unknowingly acquiesce their property rights, as the IRS surely recognizes the difference between a Tax Form and a Kind or Type of Tax.

EXM00

FORM 5564	Department of the Treasury --- Internal Revenue Service	Symbols
(Rev. June 1992)	NOTICE OF DEFICIENCY - WAIVER	Ogden 4622

Name and Address of Taxpayer(s)	January 9, 2012
▮▮▮▮▮▮▮▮	▮▮▮▮

Kind of Tax	Copy to Authorized Representative
INDIVIDUAL INCOME	

000653

Tax Year Ended	DEFICIENCY		
DECEMBER 31, 2009	Increase in Tax	$1,549.00	Penalties
	IRC Section 6651(a)(1)		348.53
	IRC Section 6651(a)(2)		147.16

I consent to the immediate assessment and collection of the deficiencies (increase in tax and penalties) shown above, plus any interest. Also, I waive the requirement under section 6532(a)(1) of the Internal Revenue Code that a notice of claim disallowance be sent to me by certified mail for any overpayment shown on the attached report. I understand that the filing of this waiver is irrevocable and it will begin the 2-year period for filing suit for refund of the claims disallowed as if the notice of disallowance had been sent by certified or registered mail.

Signature		Date
		Date
By	Title	Date

Note: If you consent to the assessment of the deficiencies shown in this waiver, please sign and return this form to limit the interest charge and expedite our bill to you. Please do not sign and return any prior notices you may have received. Your consent signature is required on this waiver, even if fully paid.

Your consent will not prevent you from filing a claim for refund (after you have paid the tax) if you later believe you are so entitled; nor prevent us from later determining, if necessary, that you owe additional tax; nor extend the time provided by law for such action.

If you later file a claim and the Service disallows it, you may file suit for refund in a District Court or in the United States Claims Court, but you may not file a petition with the United States Tax Court.

Who Must Sign: If you filed jointly, both you and your spouse must sign. Your attorney or agent may sign this waiver provided that action is specifically authorized by a power of attorney which, if not previously filed, must accompany this form.

If this waiver is signed by a person acting in a fiduciary capacity (for example, an executor, administrator, or a trustee), Form 56, Notice Concerning Fiduciary Relationship, should, unless previously filed, accompany this form.

If you agree, please sign and return this form; keep one copy for your records.

FORM 5564 (Rev. 6-92)

This is IRS Form 5564, Notice of Deficiency – Waiver, and at least it notes the Kind of Tax as an INDIVIDUAL IN-COME. However, it does not denote if it is Federal or some other jurisdiction nor does it denote the specific Tax Liability giving Rise To The Lien. They are not noting the authority or jurisdiction, so let's, just for kicks, look at IRC Section 6651(a)(1) as the form letter states as one of the reason for the Penalties.

26 U.S. Code § 6651 is Titled - Failure to file tax return or to pay tax. (a) Addition to the tax In case of failure—

to file any return required under authority of subchapter A of chapter 61 (other than part III thereof), subchapter A of chapter 51 (relating to distilled spirits, wines, and beer), or of subchapter A of chapter 52 (relating to tobacco, cigars, cigarettes, and cigarette papers and tubes), or of subchapter A of chapter 53 (relating to machine guns and certain other firearms), on the date prescribed therefor (determined with regard to any extension of time for filing), unless it is shown that such failure is due to reasonable cause and not due to willful neglect, there shall be added to the amount required to be shown as tax on such return 5 percent of the amount of such tax if the failure is for not more than 1 month, with an additional 5 percent for each additional month or fraction thereof during which such failure continues, not exceeding 25 percent in the aggregate;

So the IRS can actually charge you 5 % per month as a penalty or 25% annually. That's above usury in many States. As on a previous notation on one of the IRS forms, it appears to me this section is relating to alcohol, tobacco and firearms. This individual is a worker in private enterprise having nothing to do with these items other than having a few cocktails now and then.

Department of the Treasury
Internal Revenue Service

IRS

	SB
Notice	CP504
Tax Year	2012
Notice date	January 27, 2014
Social Security number	
To contact us	Phone
Your Caller ID	
Page 1 of 4	

Notice of intent to seize ("levy") your state tax refund or other property

Amount due immediately: $▮▮▮▮▮

As we notified you before, our records show you have unpaid taxes for the tax year ending December 31, 2012 (Form 1040). If you don't call us immediately or pay the amount due, we may seize ("levy") your property or rights to property (including any state tax refunds) and apply it to the $▮▮▮ you owe.

Billing Summary

Amount you owed	$▮▮▮
Failure-to-pay penalty	▮▮
Interest charges	▮▮
Amount due immediately	$▮▮▮

Continued on back...

IRS

Notice	CP504
Notice date	January 27, 2014
Social Security number	

Payment

- Make your check or money order payable to the United States Treasury.
- Write your Social Security number (▮▮▮▮▮ the tax year (2012), and the form number (1040) on your payment and any correspondence.

Amount due immediately $▮▮▮

INTERNAL REVENUE SERVICE

This is an IRS Form CP504, Notice of Intent to Levy and is just another one of the numerous Notices people receive in the process. You would think that this form, being an official notice, "AN INTENT TO LEVY", would provide the substantive elements of the Kind or Type of Tax being enforced against the individual, but like all the other forms, it does not.

It does note the word "taxes" but that is it. You must assume it is a tax that you are required to pay since it is from the Department of the Treasury, Internal Revenue Service. Perhaps it is also like Form 5564 relating to alcohol, tobacco and Firearms? As Citizens, we are left to only surmise what tax the Department of the Treasury, Internal Revenue Service has the authority and jurisdiction to levy and enforce against us.

What of our Taxpayer's Bill of Rights? Like much of what Congress legislates, that too, is a bunch of hogwash.

Conclusion - Material Evidence

By reviewing numerous Notice of Federal Tax Liens, we have determined that **none of the notices we found appear to have the correct Kind or Type of Tax** noted on them. Despite the requirement, by either the Federal Statutes, the United States Code, Case Law, the Internal Revenue Code, the Internal Revenue Manual and/or Treasury Regulations, we are unable to locate the Kind or Type of Tax. **The majority of the time, either they show the incorrect Kind of Tax or they show the various Sections that appear under Title 26, Internal Revenue Code.****All the NFTLs appear to be invalid, as they do not note the "Correct" Kind of Tax for the proper authority and jurisdiction to make them a legally enforceable lien.**

From all additional IRS Forms reviewed, **none of them appeared to have the correct Kind of Tax** noted on them.

Remember, according to Federal Statutes, Treasury Regulations and the Internal Revenue manual, an NFTL must note **the tax liability giving rise to the lien. Not only does the IRS "not" note the correct tax liability on the NFTLs, they do not note it on any of their forms, form letters and/or correspondences.** ****Only in those infrequent circumstances when a person may have had some Estate Income, would the person "perhaps" be liable under a 1040 Kind of Tax. As you will learn, even then, 1040 is a section in Title 26, Internal Revenue Code that is "not" Positive Law.

Since most Notice of Federal Tax Liens do not have the correct Type or Kind of Tax noted on them, they appear to be legally insufficient as Liens. Therefore they are legally invalid and should not be enforceable. As you will see however, various individuals within our government, have in my opinion been for many years perpetrating fraud and theft against the American people. What you have now been shown is the material evidence. As you will see, the following circumstantial evidence is -an additional eye opener, as it shows the blatant disregard for our rule of law by those in power. It also shows how unwilling those in power are in providing the Federal Statute(s) that they claim provides them with the authority and jurisdiction to administer and enforce the Federal Individual Income Tax.

CHAPTER 4
CIRCUMSTANTIAL EVIDENCE;
WE THE PEOPLE V. UNITED STATES
485 F.3D 140 (2007)

This renowned case, <u>which most people have never even heard of,</u> was a result of years of research and effort by some 2,000 plus people, including constitutional lawyers, academics and legal researchers headed by a very dedicated and patriotic individual by the name of Robert Schulz. I and this country owe a great deal to Bob for all that he has done and taught us. http://www.givemeliberty.org/RTPLawsuit/InfoCenter.htm and http://openjurist.org/485/f3d/140/we-the-people-foundation-inc-v-united-states

In 2002, a formal "Redress of Grievance", a right under the 1st Amendment of the Constitution, was submitted by the We the People Foundation, the group lead by Schulz, to the IRS, all 535 members of Congress, the Secretary of the Treasury and the President. Even though the IRS and one Congressman initially agreed to meet, the meeting was cancelled and no one has, **to this day**, responded nor answered the 62 questions relating to the Federal individual income tax, submitted in the formal Petition for Redress of Grievances.

In July 2004 almost 2,000 Americans, including myself, as individuals, filed a landmark lawsuit against the U.S. Government seeking to have the federal Judiciary declare -- for the first time in history -- the constitutional meaning of the 1st Amendment Petition clause including the Right of the People to enforce the Right of Petition, if Redress is denied. Sadly, a Federal Judge by the name of Emmet G. Sullivan ruled against this Constitutional right. It was then appealed, 485 F.3d 140 (2007) and in 2008 this right was again denied, this time by a three panel United States Appeals Court. It was again appealed and The Supreme Court of the United States refused to hear the case.

Another case involving the Right to Petition was a NY Supreme Court case Index No. 501776 decided in Aug. 2007, Kings Mall v. Wenk. A group of Veterans defended by the New York ACLU were again denied this Constitutional right.

Two important conclusions can be drawn from the We The People case. 1. The government just doesn't want to provide the Citizens with the Federal Statute and when it was enacted that reportedly they are using as the basis of enforcing a Federal Individual income tax on many Citizens or as many people believe, <u>there is no law,</u> and 2. We no longer have the "RIGHT" under the Constitution <u>to have our questions answered as provided under the 1st Amendment right to Petition the Government for Redress of Grievances</u>; therefore, if there is no remedy, then no such right exists and this is an obvious constitutional "Abrogation"; *transitive verb* \\'a-brə-₁gāt\\ : to end or cancel (something) in a formal and official way: to fail to do what is required: to treat as nonexistent (*abrogating their responsibilities*.) Why is there a 1st Amendment right to Petition for Redress of Grievances clause in the Constitution, if those in government can just ignore questions from the Citizens relating to the imposition, any clarifications and enforcement of our law?

Now let's look at **jurisdiction** and how important it is. Take a minute to peruse the following with emphasis on the highlights and the word <u>include(s)</u>:

The Terms "State" and "United States" Defined

#1. CITE- 26 USC Sec. 168 -EXPCITE- TITLE 26 Subtitle A CHAPTER 1 Subchapter B PART VI-HEAD- Sec. 168. Accelerated cost recovery system. For purposes of this subparagraph, the term United States' <u>includes</u> the Commonwealth of Puerto Rico and the possessions of the United States.

#2. CITE- 26 USC Sec. 217 -EXPCITE- TITLE 26 Subtitle A CHAPTER 1 Subchapter B PART
VII -HEAD- Sec. 217. Moving expenses (4) United States defined for purposes of this subsection and subsection (i), the term 'United States' <u>includes</u> the possessions of the United States.

#3. CITE-26 USC Sec. 638 Subtitle A, CHAPTER 1, Subchapter I, PART V, Sec. 638. Continental Shelf
Area (1) the term "United States" when used in a geographical sense <u>includes</u> the seabed and subsoil of those submarine areas which are adjacent to the territorial waters of the United States and over which the United States has exclusive rights, in accordance with international law, with respect to the exploration and exploitation of natural resources; and
(2) the terms "foreign country" and "possession of the United States" when used in a geographical sense <u>includes</u> the seabed and subsoil of those submarine areas which are adjacent to the territorial waters of the foreign country or such possession and over which the foreign country (or the United States in case of such possession) has exclusive rights, in accordance with international law, with respect to the exploration and exploitation of natural resources, but this paragraph shall apply in the case of a foreign country only if it exercises, directly or indirectly, taxing jurisdiction with respect to such exploration or exploitation. No foreign

country shall, by reason of the application of this section, be treated as a country contiguous to the United States.

#4. CITE- 26 USC Sec. 927 -EXPCITE- TITLE 26 Subtitle A CHAPTER 1 Subchapter N PART III Subpart C -HEAD- Sec. 927. Other definitions and special rules (3) United States defined The term 'United States' includes the Commonwealth of Puerto Rico.

#5. CITE- 26 USC Sec. 993 -EXPCITE- TITLE 26 Subtitle A CHAPTER 1 Subchapter N PART
IV Subpart A -HEAD- Sec. 993. Definitions (g) United States defined for purposes of this part, the term 'United States' includes the Commonwealth of Puerto Rico and the possessions of the United States.

#6. CITE- 26 USC Sec. 3121 -EXPCITE- TITLE 26 Subtitle C CHAPTER 21 Subchapter C -
HEAD- Sec. 3121. Definitions (2) United States The term 'United States' when used in a geographical sense includes the Commonwealth of Puerto Rico, the Virgin Islands, Guam, and American Samoa. An individual who is a citizen of the Commonwealth of Puerto Rico (but not otherwise a citizen of the United States) shall be considered, for purposes of this section, as a citizen of the United States.

#7. CITE- 26 USC Sec. 3306 -EXPCITE- TITLE 26 Subtitle C CHAPTER 23 -HEAD- Sec. 3306.
Definitions (1) State. The Term "State" includes the Commonwealth of Puerto Rico, the District of Columbia and the Virgin Islands. (2) United States The term 'United States' when used in a geographical sense includes the States, the District of Columbia,

the Commonwealth of Puerto Rico, and the Virgin Islands. An Individual who is a Citizen of the Commonwealth of Puerto Rico

#8. CITE- 26 USC Sec. 4612 -EXPCITE- TITLE 26 Subtitle D CHAPTER 38 Subchapter A -
HEAD- Sec. 4612. Definitions and special rules -STATUTE- (a) Definitions For purposes of this
subchapter (4) United States (A) In general the term 'United States' means the 50 States, the District of Columbia, the Commonwealth of Puerto Rico, any possession of the United States, the Commonwealth of the Northern Mariana Islands, and the Trust Territory of the Pacific Islands.

#9. CITE- 26 USC Sec. 7701 -EXPCITE- TITLE 26 Subtitle F CHAPTER 79 -HEAD- Sec. 7701.
Definitions (9) United States The term 'United States' when used in a geographical sense <u>includes</u> only the States and the District of Columbia. (10) State, the term 'State' shall be construed to <u>include</u> the District of Columbia, where such construction is necessary to carry out the provisions of this title.

Most people, including myself would have never guessed the number of different definitions of the term "United States" nor "State(s)" in the Internal Revenue Code. They define the different taxing jurisdictions of the United States of America by the "Federal" government.

If you carefully read the nine different definitions found, the word "<u>includes</u>" is used in all but one, and is extremely important, as you will come to see in understanding the differences between the definitions as they relate to the different jurisdictions being taxed.

From Black's Law Dictionary 6th Edition:

*"**Include.** (Lat. Inclaudere. To shut in, keep within.) To con-
fine within, hold as in an inclosure, take in, attain, shut up,
contain, inclose, comprise, comprehend, embrace, involve.
Term may, according to context, express an enlargement
and have the meaning of and or in addition to, or merely
specific a particular thing already included within general
words therefore used.....* **"Including" within the statute, is
interpreted as a word of enlargement or of illustrated application as well as a word of limitation."**

As will become self-evident from analyzing the definitions, as it relates to the issue of jurisdiction(s) being taxed, the
various uses of the word "include(s)" in the various definitions
always relates to a word of **limitation.** You will see in every case
the term "include(s)" is used as a term of limitation, limiting the
definition to only the specific jurisdictions noted after the word.
What we are trying to evaluate and determine is if any of the definitions in the Internal Revenue Code create a jurisdiction for the
Federal Individual Income Tax on Citizens of the 50 States.

A way to evaluate and understand this is to take the different definitions from the previous list of known jurisdictions cited
in the Internal Revenue Code and place them into specific catego-
ries and situations. As an example, Puerto Rico is a unique part of
the United States because it is treated as a State in certain circumstances, yet most of its Citizens, as you will see later on, are not
required to participate in the Federal Individual Income Tax system, as are allegedly the Citizens of the 50 States and the District
of Columbia. Most of the Citizens of Puerto Rico only pay a personal income tax to the Government of Puerto Rico and not to the
Federal Government of the United States when they have income
from within Puerto Rico. Therefore when looking at the various
definitions, #8 cannot be the definition for the Federal Individual

Income Tax because it includes Puerto Rico as a State and they are not required to pay a Federal Individual Income Tax.

The District of Columbia (DC), another Federal jurisdiction as you will see later in a Supreme Court case, **Hooven & Allison Co vs. Evatt,324 U.S.652 (1945),** is in fact under the legislative purview of Congress. However, when Congress is legislating for one of its Federal jurisdictions such as the District of Columbia or in the Hooven & Allison case, the *Philippines*, it is not bound by the same constitutional limitation as when they are legislating for the 50 States. There are several reasons that this came about and deals often with the military, national defense and security issues.

The Citizens living and working in the District of Columbia have Congress as their legislative body and even has their own courts, Mayor and Council much like any other city. http://en.wikipedia.org/wiki/United_States_territorial_court and http://en.wikipedia.org/wiki/Washington,_D.C.

In definition #9, notice that it does not include Puerto Rico as a State, but only the District of Columbia, so it could potentially be the definition for the IRS taxing jurisdiction as it relates to the Federal Individual Income Tax since the Citizens of Puerto Rico do no participate in that tax. However, since the District of Columbia is also taxed as a state, this definition is the only one that includes just the District of Columbia and excludes everything else as a state, thus this by default must be a tax similar to other State Income Taxes for those that live and work in the District of Columbia, because they also pay a Federal Income Tax in addition to the tax paid to the District of Columbia. I am aware of this because my niece is an Attorney working and living in DC, or at least was, and paid close to 50% in total Income taxes to the Federal government and DC.

Many people believe and the IRS attempts to use this definition of the State in §7701 of the IRC to include the 50 States. This is not logical however, because the District of Columbia must have its own jurisdiction within the IRC, independent and exclusive of all others and this definition is the only one that appears to incorporate just the District of Columbia, exclusive of all others. Suggesting that this includes the 50 States, even though the "50 States" or any of the prior defined States such as Puerto Rico or the American Virgin Islands are defined as a State, when they are not "included" is the definition is illogical. It also stays consistent on the issue of "includes" being a term of limitations. In the definition, the term State only includes the District of Columbia.

In #6, the definition does "include" the 50 States, the District of Columbia and Puerto Rico. Since everyone knows Puerto Rico does not pay a Federal Individual Income tax, #6 could not be the definition for the jurisdiction of the Federal Individual Income Tax either, because Puerto Rico is included and they are not required to file and pay this tax.

As you can clearly see, the various definitions show that "includes" relate to a term of limitation. Puerto Rico is included in #1, #4, #5, #6, #7 and #8 and excluded from #2 and #9. Note that number #4 says that the Commonwealth of Puerto Rico and the "possessions" of the United States are different jurisdictions which would result in Puerto Rico not being considered a Possession of the United States, and thus would therefore exclude #2 from relating to Puerto Rico.

Both #7 and #9 are interesting because they do not incorporate the phrase "the 50 States" as does #8 yet both have the definition of States but they exclude the phrase "the 50 States" and specify which jurisdictions they do "include".

To me, the definitions are very specific and consistent as to what they include and exclude. Surely if Congress wanted to include "the 50 States" in any of those definitions they would have done so. Therefore the intention of the lawmakers is obvious, in that they consistently use the term "includes" as a word of limitation. Why have the various definitions been so specific if they can be construed as words of enlargement? It would be irrational to conclude that say in #9, it could also include Puerto Rico or some other jurisdiction because it is considered a State in certain circumstances, such as it is in #7. Under that rationale we could be taxed by the State we live in as well as when Congress is legislating for the Territories or any one of its other jurisdictions. As it relates to Tax Jurisdictions within the IRC, "includes" is obviously a word of limitation.

Now here's the kicker and why the word "includes" is so important. Not one of the jurisdictions being taxed, as noted by the various definitions of such, in the entire Internal Revenue Code appear to "include" the 50 States, the District of Columbia and "exclude" the Commonwealth of Puerto Rico as a taxing jurisdiction, which would be required for the Federal Individual Income Tax to be applicable to that jurisdiction. Thus, it provides additional circumstantial evidence as to both the lack of a specific Federal Individual Income Tax Statute but also why the Kinds of Tax noted on the NFTLs are incorrect.

From the IRS website: http://www.irs.gov/taxtopics/tc901.html

Topic 901 - Is a Person With Income From Puerto Rican Sources Required to File a U.S. Federal Income Tax Return?

*In general, United States citizens and resident aliens who are bona fide residents of Puerto Rico during the **entire** tax year, which for most individuals is January 1 to December*

*31, __are not required to file a U.S. federal income tax re-__
__turn if they have income only from sources within Puerto__
__Rico__. If they have income from sources outside of Puerto
Rico, including within the 50 states or the District of Columbia, or if they are employees of the U.S. government,
they are required to file a U.S. federal income tax return.
Bona fide residents of Puerto Rico generally do not report
income received from sources within Puerto Rico on their
U.S. income tax return.*

Note that they also *always* use the phrase "50 States" when
specifying all the States of the Union. Many pro tax people claim
that my #9, CITE- 26 USC Sec. 7701 is the definition where the
jurisdiction for the Federal Individual Income tax is specified. In
light of the preceding analysis, that is not logical because it does
not specify the 50 States which it must. It only defines a State to
include the District of Columbia and excludes all of the other taxing jurisdictions, including the 50 States. It appears to me the IRS
does not have taxing authority over most Citizens of the 50 States,
unless they live in the District of Columbia. But, as I have previously written, the IRS must still note the tax liability giving rise
to the lien on their NFTLs for them to be valid. Instead they play
these word games and various other fraudulent and manipulative
tactics to coerce Citizens of the 50 States to file and pay a Federal
Individual Income Tax.

Assumptions about Collection Fraud

Now we are going to look at "Why" this might be happening and "Why" the IRS does not correctly note the Kind of Tax
on the various documentation and NFTL's provided by them during the collection and enforcement process. Since you cannot
prove a law doesn't exist, we can then, only supply circumstantial

evidence as support for what appears to be the reason. It appears, as the Tax Honesty Movement and the following information will show, there doesn't appear to have been a Federal Statute that has ever been enacted into law. This would be an obvious potential reason as to why the IRS does not note the correct Kind of Tax on the NFTLs and why they "Refused" to answer the formal Petition for Redress of Grievance. This is why almost all Notice of Federal Tax Lien(s) filed at the local county courthouses around our nation are thus defective. They fail to properly note the correct "kind of **Tax liability giving rise to the Lien**".

What appears to have taken place is that the IRS issues an erroneous substitute for the "Kind of Tax" on the NTFL, in an attempt to enforce their ***non-existent*** taxing powers, hoping the Citizens will not rise up in mass and stop them from taking such actions. So far they have been successful. I call it fraudulent, because if I was able to figure all this out, someone at the IRS, Treasury and Justice Departments surely knows this, and if not, they should. Ignorance is no excuse under the law, especially if this is your specific job.

Title 26 is "Not" Positive Law

Here is another reason why, and the evidence "I believe", the IRS is fraudulently assessing most people for 1040, 941 Kind of Taxes and the others previous noted penalties and not from a specific Section(s) within Title 26, Internal Revenue Code and Title 27, Alcohol Tobacco and Firearms, that denotes a true tax.

As you can see Title 26, according to paragraph 3 below, from the "Government Printing Office (GPO)", is excluded and therefore it is **"Not"** positive law. This is also common knowledge among Constitutional scholars and those who study and research Tax Law. Title 27, Alcohol Tobacco and Firearms is also "not" Positive Law. This is important because since they are not positive law titles they can only be used as prima fascia evidence in a court of law. In reference to a specific law, prima fascia evidence really doesn't apply. Prima Fascia means on its face; on the first appearance; so far as can be judged from the first disclosure; at first sight; a fact presumed to be true unless disproved by some evidence to the contrary, Prima Fascia Evidence is evidence which if unexplained or not contradicted, is sufficient to sustain a judgment in favor of the issue which it supports, but which may be contradicted by other evidence. – Black's Law Dictionary Sixth Addition. Either a law exists or it doesn't.

Why is this important? The IRS has tried in the past to claim that the various Sections in Title 26, Internal Revenue Code are prima fascia evidence. This however can be contradicted in a Court of Law. Either the law exists or it doesn't exist. The IRC is a compilation of all the tax laws ever passed by Congress since the origin of our Republic. For a law to be in the IRC it must have been passed sometime in our nation's history. The IRS tries to say that the IRC is prima Fascia Evidence and this is satisfactory as evidence for their authority. Since Title 26 is not positive law, it **cannot** be treated as such and therefore they must show the specific Act and when it was passed as real evidence of its existence. It *appears* that the law exists? No, it either does or it doesn't.

About the United States Code from:

http://www.gpo.gov/help/about_united_states_code.htm
"1. The U.S. Code (USC) is the codification by subject matter of the general and permanent laws of the United States. It is divided by broad subjects into 51 titles and published by the Office of the Law Revision Counsel of the U.S. House of Representatives. The U.S. Code was first published in

1926. The next main edition was published in 1934, and subsequent main editions have been published every six years since 1934. In between editions, annual cumulative supplements are published in order to present the most current information.

2. FDsys contains virtual main editions of the U.S. Code. The information contained in the U.S. Code on FDsys has been provided to GPO by the Office of the Law Revision Counsel of the U.S. House of Representatives. While every effort has been made to ensure that the U.S. Code database on FDsys is accurate, those using it for legal research should verify their results against the printed version of the U.S. Code available through the Government Printing Office.

3. Of the 51 titles, the following titles have been enacted into positive (statutory) law: 1, 3, 4, 5, 9, 10, 11, 13, 14, 17, 18, 23, 28, 31, 32, 35, 36, 37, 38, 39, 40, 41, 44, 46, 49, and 51. When a title of the Code is enacted into positive law, the text of the title becomes legal evidence of the law. Titles that have not been enacted into positive law are only prima facie evidence of the law. In that case, the Statutes at Large still govern.

4. The U.S. Code does not include regulations issued by executive branch agencies, decisions of the Federal courts, treaties, or laws enacted by State or local governments. Regulations issued by executive branch agencies are available in the Code of Federal Regulations. Proposed and recently adopted regulations may be found in the Federal Register."

THE TERM "POSITIVE LAW"

Here is the website URL for the Office of the Law Revision Council (OLRC), United States House of Representatives. - http://uscode.house.gov/codification/term_positive_law.htm

You can read about Positive Law for yourself, because of its length, to examining why Title 26 and Tile 27 are "Not" positive law. As analyzed previously, the jurisdictions that each law in Title 26 are written for, therefore becomes very important as to the relevance of laws specified in the Title. As you've seen Congress enacts legislation for at least nine (9) different jurisdictions that were found in the IRC.

This does not present evidence, as we saw with the different definitions, of the existence of a specific law that requires Citizens of the 50 States to pay a Federal Individual Income Tax on their labor, in their individual capacity. Some believe it is Chapter 1 Subtitle A Section 1 of Title 26, but this Section once evaluated does not appear to be that law because, as you saw, the jurisdiction, as noted in Section 7701, does not include the 50 States but only the District of Columbia.

What it OLRC does provide us, is that the 1939, 1954 and 1986 Congressional enactments of the Internal Revenue Code by Congress still **did not make Title 26 "Positive Law".** I'm not sure of the reasons and several theories exist for readers to explore.

Once again, we can only assume why such actions have occurred over the last century. Why are Title 26, our so-called Federal Individual Income Tax law and Title 27, Alcohol, Tobacco and Firearms, "NOT" considered by the United States House of Representatives to be Positive Law? There could be a variety of reasons, but none of them substantiate the existence of a specific Statute for the purpose of taxing the private labor of Citizens of the 50 States enacted by Congress anytime in our history.

Once again, it doesn't really matter that much but it just becomes additional circumstantial evidence to support the lack of any identifying Statute(s) on the Notice of Federal Tax Liens.

So…. the key is, proving if **a Citizen of the United States of America's labor, when reporting income as an individual taxpayer,** is liable for a Federal Individual Income Tax or "not". This still depends on if a Federal Statute/Law has ever been enacted that requires Citizens to do so. For those that study tax law, they understand there is an extensive reason, once again, too long for this book, of why the underlined wording above is so important. The majority of Citizens do not, in my opinion, fall under this category of "Taxpayers" under Title 26, Internal Revenue Code.

Has such a law ever been enacted? Is there an actual Federal Statute, passed by Congress that specifically sets forth the various regulatory elements required for it to be positive law? What this does, is place the burden of proof on our government to either prove or disprove that a tax as defined above, has ever been enacted into law.

Since it is impossible to supply evidence that such a law "does not" exist, it therefore can only be proven by showing that a specific "Act" of Congress was approved and passed by both Houses and then signed by the then President of the United States, for it to be "Positive Law". Thus the burden of proof lies on the Government.

That is the only way to prove that a specific portion of Title 26, has been enacted and thus is positive law. **Just show We The People Foundation and the rest of the Citizens of the United States of America the Law and the subject could be** put to rest. **For some unknown reason, no one from the Government is willing to show us the law!**

      There are at least **"four"** things that I and others in the Tax Honest movement are aware of on the following issues. **Are most Citizens of the United States of America, liable for Federal Individual Income Tax on their labor when reporting income as an individual taxpayer?** I need to add one caveat here; The Code of Federal Regulations does note that individuals when participating "in the performance of the functions of a public office" are under the Jurisdiction of the Federal Government and that certain individuals who are involved with certain products/objects are also under Federal jurisdiction, appear to be the exceptions. I would think that such products as plutonium and many military hardware/weapons would fall under the Jurisdiction of the Federal Government.

What "WE" Know:

    1. First, no one I've ever spoken or written to, who I have ever asked this question to has **ever** been able to show me the specific Federal Statute and when it was passed that requires the above. Nor, has anyone that I've ever challenged to do this, ever been able to show me or anyone else the specific Congressional Act and when it was passed, not one.

    2. Second, many individuals have requested to be shown the specific Federal Statute and when it was enacted and not once has the IRS or any other entity within the Federal Government provided it. Many people including myself have not only sent Certified Mail Return Requests, but also filed Freedom of Information Act (FOIA) requests asking this very question. No Agency of the Government has ever responded to these requests that I've ever seen,

and I and others have been requesting this information for over thirty (30) years.

3. Additionally, a formal "Redress of Grievance" with Constitutional scholars and Tax Attorneys involved in its preparation, as afforded by the 1st Amendment to the Constitution; *".... and to petition the Government for redress of grievances"*, was submitted by We The People Foundation on April 15, 2002 to the various entities including the IRS, Treasury Department, DOJ, all members of Congress and the President of the United States. This was repeated multiple times to ensure proper notice. All entities and individuals within the Government ignored the Petition which included if the specific statute existed (Question #58). We the People then sued the government to force an answer to the questions, and low and behold, the Federal Judges ruled that the Government is not required to answer a formal Petition for Redress of Grievances. Are you starting to see a pattern of **nobody within the government wanting to answer what should be a fairly simply group of questions and that many people down the chain of authority within the Federal Government are complicit, whether they know it or not.** http://www.givemeliberty.org/FreedomDrive/Redress/PETITIONtax.pdf

4. There is a growing list of ex-IRS agents, Tax Attorneys, accountants, CPAs, other tax professionals and millions of Citizens that believe the government, specifically the IRS and Federal Judges, in collusion, are enforcing a law that has never been enacted.

CHAPTER 5
ME AND THE IRS; NEVER AN ANSWER

When accepting the Democratic Party's nomination for President in 1976, the next President of the United States, Jimmy Carter stated, "It is time for a complete overhaul of our income tax system. I still tell you: <u>it is a disgrace to the human race.</u> All my life I have heard promises about tax reform, but it never quite happens."

"A heavy progressive or graduated income tax", as written by the infamous Karl Max and Richard Engels, in their book "The Communist Manifesto", <u>is the 2nd platform of their communist manifesto. The ten platforms can be found on pages 74 and 75 of the "A Norton Critical Edition" published by W.W. Norton and Company.</u>

I believe, for the wealthy and politically powerful through cronyism, to tax the individual labor of the middle classes and poor of their societies, when there are numerous other ways to tax that are much fairer in their effects upon the human experience, is both <u>UNCONSCIONABLE and DISGRACEFUL.</u>

It was late 1986 and early 1987 when I first recognized that the Internal Revenue Service and I had a problem. I had been railroaded out of a small boutique investment banking firm, keeping $42,000 in my commissions. The money owed to me obviously their incentive for my desk being cleared off one day when I came to work. This is important because I had concluded one and three quarter years of work with a low salary draw against commissions, as I was a commissioned independent contractor, much like a real estate agent. I tried to sue, but any potential assets were nowhere to be found and with no money on the potential table, no Attorney would finalize the suit.

The following year the two partners and I started a new S-Corp and netted $75,000 with each getting $25,000 as individual income. This is when I began to realize how unjust the Federal Income Tax system was.

The partners had all worked hard that year, often times on weekends and we had done fairly well under the circumstances, because part of our profits came from residential mortgage originations, which was a new venture for all three of us.

I was divorced with two young children. I took no vacations, hardly even a weekend off. I had to drive to Atlanta to pick up the kids whenever I could afford it, keeping them most of the summers, doing several weekend round trips of over 1,400 miles.

I didn't buy myself any new cloths or anything much else, because I just couldn't afford it. Thank goodness my mother helped me out, even though she wasn't in much better financial shape. I did a budget and I was actually operating in the red. Low income two bedroom rents back then were $625 a month. I managed my parent's apartment complex, also barely breaking even, thus having to repair, collect rents and evict people, etc. on my nights and days off. I was, in my opinion, living at a below poverty lifestyle, with a $25,000 income level and working my tail off. I was actually caring for my Mom and a younger disabled brother as well, as my parents had just divorced.

As the tax season rolled around, with my wife getting the child deductions in the divorce, I found that with all the allowable deductions, my tax liability was still about $2,500, which of course, I didn't have, nor could get or really afford. I couldn't even afford to pay an accountant, so I just didn't file and pay that year nor had I paid the previous year, thinking that they cannot get blood out of a stone, nor did I have any assets that they could seize.

Low and behold, my greatest fear became a reality, the IRS came calling, even coming to my office despite this being illegal, to speak with me and try to get me to sign tax returns that "they" had prepared. I signed them just to get the guy off my back. I ended up having $1,000 seized from my bank account a year or so later, that I needed for paying my bills and child support, etc. My child support Magistrate, a female, wondered why I didn't pay my child support and put me in jail, despite my having told her the story and provided the evidence.

After that, I didn't hear anything until early 1990, when the IRS called me into the local office, where I got to meet my IRS agent. In the meantime however, I started getting familiar with the Tax Honesty Movement where I came to realize there was this huge movement of people who believed that the US Constitution protected most individuals from being taxed on their individual labor when they worked for somebody else or as an employee or self-employed in a non-corporate status. It's a little more complicated than that, but I believed and still do, that I, as a Citizen of one of the 50 States, was not involved in a taxable "privileged" occupation nor was involved in a business or businesses with products or objects taxable under Federal Jurisdiction. The Tax Honest Movement believed and still does, that the Income Tax Act of 1913 relates to "business" income on labor in a Corporate Capacity, which after reviewing the Congressional discussions on the issue, appeared correct to me.

The meeting with the IRS Agent was relatively brief and after explaining my positions, his comment was "you really do believe in what you are saying" and then I said "well, so what's next?". What came out of his mouth next was a little surprising; "probably nothing", and upon hearing that, I could not get out the examination room and front door of the IRS offices fast enough.

I have had no major exchanges with them after that period, but I must tell you, that before this time, I had replied to every letter, notice and telephone call from them. I have spent voluminous hours doing this and have always asked the same basic questions, some that are part of this book.

It wasn't until many years later, after reviewing several Notice of Federal Tax Liens from friends and associates, that I noticed and discovered the primary material evidence of this book.

The various letters and notices I received, as well as others, never had the Kind of Tax noted on them. Obviously, this raised a big "RED" flag and one of the reasons why I keep asking for the specific Federal Statute and when it was passed on all correspondence with the IRS.

Additionally, I would always ask for the specific definition of "Income" they are using, knowing that Income had always been heavily fought over in the Courts with a vast array of opinions. From all the appellate decisions I've read over the years, in my opinion, it would be hard to make a conclusive definition of "Income". This is important, because the IRS Code itself does not define the term "income" as a single word, but only "gross income". From studying accounting, "Gross Income" is a business term, which gave credence to the belief that the Income Tax Act of 1913 was not a tax on individual income, but from a business position, although the government tries to always skirt this issue. It wasn't the individual employee being taxed but the company who was receiving gross income from labor, it was selling. As an example, when I worked with my father, we provided home furnishings such as, wallpaper to clients. We also of course provided the wallpaper installation and if they already had their own wallpaper, we provided just the installation at 50% higher than what it cost us. Back then, our cost for wallpaper installation was about $10.00 a roll, which included the wall paper hanger's labor, their materials such as the paste, tools, transportation, etc.; these being the costs of providing this service. We would turn around and sell this service at $15.00 per roll, for a $5.00 or 50% profit. Is the $5.00 taxable? No, because we have additional costs and expenses associated with our business, just like the wallpaper hangers have their expenses against what they are charging for their service.

The issue was not the money that Lenny and Wayne, the wallpaper father and son installation team received from their labor for just installing the wallpaper, it was my father and his company's income on their labor that was the issue of the Act, as it applied to a business corporation. As you can understand, the various issues can be a little confusing. I used this example, because if you don't think it is even difficult for Congresspersons and Judges to wrap their heads around the various issues, many being much more complicated, you are sadly mistaken. By reading the Congressional records, which detail the various discussions and speeches during the debates on the House and Senate Bills in 1913, the questions and statements are evidence of this.

If you want to read all the committee and legislative debates, this is where you would start. It could be a book in and of itself. http://www.archives.gov/legislative/guide/house/chapter-23-joint-internal-revenue-taxation.html

When the significance of what was going on finally came to me, a year or so ago, is when we had asked what a "1040" Kind of Tax was, as well as various other questions relating to the tax, after a request for a CDP hearing by a friend on their NFTL. The interesting part was the Title of the letter and the response; Titled:

"Appeals is disregarding your request for a Collection Due Process and/or Equivalent Hearing."

The person wrote: "I am disregarding your request for a Due Process and/or Equivalent Hearing, because I have determined that your disagreement is either:

a "specific frivolous position" identified by the IRS in Notice 2006-14 (for Notice 2006-14, refer to the website at http://www.irs.gov/newsroom/article/0,,id=177519.00.html or

a reason that is not a specific frivolous position, "but is a frivolous reason reflecting a desire to delay or impede federal tax, administer; or a moral, religious, political, constitutional, conscientious, or

similar objection to impede the administration of federal tax laws. Collection may proceed with collection action as if the hearing request was never submitted."

Once we received this letter, we knew that an even larger red flag had just appeared, as we had not actually made any claims, frivolous or not, nor were or could we physically impede their enforcement. We had stated that we just wanted to ask various questions pertaining to the law, so that my friend could determine their tax liability, if any. Once again, we could not get our questions answered.

I had gone through the entire ordeal with We The People vs the United States lawsuit so I was already very familiar with the lack of response from various government entities regarding the various questions on the Federal Individual Income Tax or whatever it is called. As an interesting note, the only place that I've ever seen, from the IRS, any other entity of the Government or any of its representatives, actually to give the full or proper name of the tax they are enforcing is on the 1040 filing Form itself.

Back in the beginning, I just started replying in writing, either certified or return receipt request, with questions when I got notices and letters from the IRS. I've always kept in mind that there may not be a law, as those in the tax honesty movement believed, that requires most people to pay a Federal Individual Income tax on their individual labor because first and foremost, no one would or had ever showed it to me and this claim still applies at this very moment.

Remembering this, I've always tried to be respectful, sincere and succinct in my responses to the IRS and just kept asking questions. Generally, I never made any claims, except once on the advice of another individual who showed me evidence that he had some success against with the IRS. Myself and others have responded at least 20, maybe even 25 or more times to different notices and letters from the IRS, always asking the same basic questions: please provide the Federal Statute, when it was passed, the definition of income, what is a 1040 or Kind of Tax being referred to, etc. Additionally I would ask for all the information they have, that would make them believe that I'm a "Taxpayer" as they define it, all the information that they have on me regarding this tax, etc. The reason for some of the questions are important and interesting, although moot from the aspect of the validity and enforcement of the NFTL. These can be found in numerous books on the subject.

NOT THE IRS, OR ANY OTHER GOVERNMENT AGENCY, OR INDIVIDUAL REPRESENTING THEM, HAS EVER RESPONDED TO ANY OF MY/OUR REQUESTS FOR INFORMATION OR HAVE EVER ANSWERED MY/OUR QUESTIONS. WHY?

As I mentioned in my personal story with the IRS, I have, on numerous occasions requested various pieces of information from the IRS including a request for information via a Freedom of Information Act request (FOIA) always sent by either Return Receipt Request or Certified Mail. I suggest always doing this when corresponding with any government agency and always in writing.

The following two pages are a typical letter that I have sent to the IRS asking the same basic questions.

One can only assume that the reason they do not wish to disclose such pertinent information is that it would give everyone the needed knowledge to legally avoid the tax since Tax Evasion is illegal and tax avoidance is not. If there is no law, I guarantee everyone would legally avoid this tax, based on its non-existence.

Legal Analysis, 16th Amendment

This is primarily the opinion of William (Bill) Tinnerman. He is a friend, great person, patriot and he is also fearless.

"The IRS/SB-SE Division NFTL claim on behalf of the United States Government is procedurally deficient pursuant to a delegation requirement to promulgate obligatory regulations under sections 6001 and 6011 of the I.R.C. [68A Stat 1, as amended (Code)] specifically applied in most cases relevant to IRC Subtitle A, Chapter 1, Subchapter A, Part I "Individuals", whether "domestic" or "foreign" - all undefined "terms" in the Code, affecting the lawfulness of any administrative 6212 deficiency determination and 6323(f) lien "notice" arising there from, as well as, a requirement to promulgate obligatory regulations under the Administrative Procedures Act (APA), codified at 5 U.S.C. 552(a)(1), which substantive regulations under either statute do not exist relevant to "all receipts" of any "Citizen" domiciled or doing business in the "United (50) States" *, and thereby not perfected and "ripe" as a matter of law, which prohibits any court (State, Federal or Bankruptcy) to have jurisdiction to sustain such a claim. (also see Tax Court Rule 13(a)).

Any Court Order sustaining a claim without verification of the substantive regulatory obligation required by statute specific to the party the claim applies, such subject-jurisdiction of the court can be challenged [535 U.S. 625 (2002)] and if sustained, the Court Order issued is void.

*Note: "all receipts", "Citizen(s)" and "United (50) States" are all constitutionally derived words, either by the instrument or the Supreme Court, and pursuant to Eisner at 205-207 the "excise" tax authorized by the 16th amendment was not affected (see Brushaber at 17-19) and Congress via its' legislative power cannot alter this!

In other words, without a Federal Regulation, there is no right for any court to enforce the collection, as all U.S. Courts lack jurisdiction to even hear a Case involving IRS collections against Citizens of the 50 States. It sure does take a lot of legalese to state what should be common sense. You can't enforce a law that doesn't exist.

Until such time as someone who is a United States Government Official shows the Citizens the law and answers the sixty two (62) questions, the Citizens of the country appear to have NO alternative but to assume that no such Federal Regulation exists.

Conclusion from Circumstantial Evidence

As is self-evident, the fraud begins when the amount of the assessment is determined under an erroneous Kind of Tax and then, when the Notice of Federal Tax Lien is both created by the IRS and then issued to and recorded in the Country Records by the Clerks of Court around the Country, subjecting various Citizens to the, lien, levy and collection. As we have seen, the fraud is evidenced on the Notice of Federal Tax Liens, under the Kind of Tax incorrectly noted in column (a) and therefore each previous action prior to the filing of the fraudulent NFTL is also a fraudulent action because they lack authority and jurisdiction.

First however, we must consider and notify if necessary, the actual individual(s) in the IRS, doing the calculations and the individual(s) in charge and doing the assessments and make 100% sure they are knowingly aware of the facts about the fraud. Some individual(s) within the IRS may just be doing what they have been taught to do and may not necessarily know that they are actually committing a crime by created a fraudulent document and thus a fraud against various Citizens.

Once they are notified though and shown the evidence of what they are doing and why, either they are going to have to stop or be complicit in the conspiracy. That list is already long enough. It's important to note that those who already know or will be shown the evidence, if they number two or more individuals, is the definition of conspiracy.

The more notifications that are sent to the various people, the more pressure there will be on them to stop, and if they don't stop they are no longer protected by what is called sovereign immunity. As long as a government employee is operating within their lawful authority, they are protected from prosecution, however once they knowingly are committing a fraud, as would be in the case once they are noticed, this opens the door to not only suing the IRS, Treasury Officials, Justice Officials, and the Clerks of Court, but the specific individual IRS agents involved.

Not only do we have the specific evidence of a fraud within the Notice of Federal Tax Liens as well as other required IRS documentation by those in official government positions, via filing invalid NFTLs, we also have several pieces of circumstantial and material evidence to support both the unlawful enforcement and confiscation of property from Citizens. We also have material evidence that our Constitution has and continues to be abrogated by various Prosecutors from the Justice Department and Federal Judges.

Since the IRS has been totally uncooperative on these issues, this therefore can only be a hypothesis, based on the evidence and analysis of the book. So let's review what we do know.

The evidence presented clearly shows that the "Kind of Tax" being assessed against most people via the Notice of Federal Tax Lien (NFTL) is either a tax on income from an estate based on Title 26, §1040 and some other "unknown" Sections within the code, even though in the interviews and research undertaken, there had been no income received by the individuals of that kind i.e., being an Estate Tax.

The Notice of Federal Tax Lien (NFTL) in column (a) notes "Kind of Tax" and therefore 1040 logically cannot represent a Tax Form. It would have to note "Kind of Form" instead of "Kind of Tax" on the NFTL if that were the case.

No one I've have ever met, seen, heard of or spoken to has ever seen the specific Federal Statute and when it was passed?

The IRS, nor anyone from the government, have provided or shown the "alleged" Federal Statute to Citizens nor has the Judiciary been willing to force the government to answer the various questions regarding the law, specifically Questions #58 – #62, of the formal Petition Redress of Grievances noted in the prior Chapter. This unwillingness and failure to provide the alleged Federal Statute and provide the answers to the specific questions to those that have requested it, in the various available methods, is the greatest indictment of the truth. If it existed wouldn't they just show it to everyone and answer the friggin questions!!!!! They must not be able to and one can only conclude that therefore, it obviously doesn't exist.

It appears with a high level of certainty that there are numerous individuals in government, including Judges that are deliberately and intentionally denying Citizens the protection of their individual rights and property and therefore are co-conspirators in a fraudulent tax scheme to literally "steal" money from Citizens. This is well documented, not only here, but in a vast number of law suits over many years including the We the People Foundation's Right to Petition for Redress of Grievances case. Sadly for many, the testimonial list of people who have been subjected to the unlawful enforcement of the Federal Individual Income tax is vast. Isn't it time we stand up and stop the corruption.

CHAPTER 6
WORDS, TERMS AND CASE HISTORIES

Definitions:

From Black's Law Dictionary, Sixth Edition
Abrogate: To annul, cancel, revoke, repeal or destroy.
Fraud: An intentional perversion of truth for the purpose of inducing another in reliance upon it to part some valuable thing belonging to them or to surrender a legal right.
Treason: The offense of attempting by overt acts to overthrow the government of the state to which the offender owes allegiance. Treason consists of two elements: adherence to the enemy and rendering him aid and comfort. A person can be convicted of treason on the testimony of two witnesses or confession in open court.
Overt Act: An open, manifest act from which criminality may be implied. An outward act done in pursuance and manifestation of an intent or design.
Insurrection: Consists in any combined resistance to the lawful authority of the State, with intent to cause the denial of such.
Usurpation: The unlawful encroachment or assumption of the use of property, power or authority which belongs to another.
FYI: I used Black's Law, Sixth Addition, because it is one of the most commonly used dictionaries in law.

The Oath of Office

The Oath of Office is not only a crucial element of the Constitution, the President, Vice President, all members of Con-

gress, all Judges and all commissioned and even non-commis-
sioned military personnel are required by statute to   I
_____ *"do solemnly swear, that they will support and defend the Constitution of the United States against all **enemies, foreign and domestic**: that they will bear true faith and allegiance
to the same, that they take this obligation freely, without any men-
tal reservation or purpose of evasion: So help them God.*

Using just the definitions above, one could make the case
and argument that allowing the various abrogation's of our Constitution to take place and the usurpations of rights, in this case
the usurpation of "property rights" through fraud has occurred,
because various individuals are breaking their Oath of Office. The
problem is that those who could prosecute those offenders are either the ones participating in the fraud or working in collusion
with them. We also know what can happen to whistle blowers and
rebellious types.

Jurisdiction Explained

It is important to understand a little about the term jurisdiction because of the way U.S. law and our justice system works.
The Citizens of the 50 States cannot assume that all laws passed
by Congress or other political bodies apply to them because laws
are passed that apply to different jurisdictions and Citizenships.

It has a very lengthy definition but it is basically according
to Blacks Law, Sixth Edition *"the legal right by which Judges
exercise their authority." and "Areas of authority, the geographic
area in which a court has power or type of cases it has power to
hear."*

Congress for instance, may pass laws that apply to just
military activities or the District of Columbia, or Puerto Rico, or

the 50 States and DC in combination, etc. A specific Court must have the authority to hear such cases in the various jurisdictions.

A military Court hears military cases, but sometimes a civilian court may hear a case involving military operations if the civil court is deemed to have jurisdiction. How do we know when Congress is passing a law that applies to a specific jurisdiction? Simply, the law, for it to be Constitutional must note the jurisdiction it applies to. The case below is an example.

Hooven & Allison Co vs. Evatt,324 U.S.652 (1945)

(When legislating for the Federal Zone (In this case the Philippines)) Congress is not subject to the same constitutional limitations, as when it is legislating for the United States....And in general the guarantees of the Constitution, save as they are limitations on the exercise of executive and legislative power when exerted for or over our insular possessions, extend to them only as Congress, in the exercise of its legislative power over the territory belonging to the United States, has made those guaranties applicable.

In another recent case involving the 2nd Amendment, here is what the Plaintiff's council said about the Judge's decision: *"Evidently, at least in Judge Walton's opinion, citizens living within the Washington, D.C. city limits do not enjoy the same constitutional rights as citizens living in neighboring Maryland, Virginia or any of the other fifty states," Gottlieb added. "Just where is the warning sign on the road leading into the nation's capitol telling citizens that 'beyond this point, the Constitution is null and void'?*

This opinion was thankfully appealed and the SCOTUS "somehow" got it right and reversed this opinion.

I am expounding on the term "Jurisdiction" for both an educational purpose and to show you just how important it is, not to just assume if a law does or does not exist and just as important even if it exists, does it apply to the proper or correct jurisdiction(s) we believe it to. We as Citizens really do have to understand jurisdiction so that we can be assured which laws apply to us and which laws may not.

Here is an Appellate Case to put this point into further perspective:

> *"It is clear that Congress, as a legislative body, exercise <u>two species of legislative power</u>: the one, limited as to its objects, but extending all over the Union: the other, an absolute, exclusive legislative power over the District of Columbia. The preliminary inquiry in the case now before the Court, is, by virtue of which of these authorities was the law in question passed?" Cohens v. Virginia, 19 U.S. 264, 6 Wheat. 265; 5 L.Ed. 257 (1821)*

You'll see later, why I believe jurisdiction is so important to understanding how the Government is enforcing the Federal Individual Income Tax.

Citizenship - Two Different Types?
and important 14th Amendment Cases;

First though, I thought that it would be interesting to define for educational purposes, the term "Citizen". Some Tax Honesty folks contend that there are two different types of Citizens in this Country because of the 14th Amendment and jurisdiction plays a relevant part in the definitions.

Understand that it can be either the Legislature and/or the Judiciary that defines words and terms.

The court said: "There is, then, under our republican form of government, two classes of citizens, one of the United

States and one of the state. Once class of citizenship may exist in a person without the other, as in the case of a resident of the District of Columbia; but **both classes usually exist in the same person.** *The federal government by this amendment (the 14th amendment) has undertaken to say who shall be a citizen of both the states and the United States. "The rights and privileges, and immunities which the fourteenth constitutional amendment and Rev. St. Section 1979 [U.S. Comp. St. 1901, p. 1262], for its enforcement, were designated to protect, are such as belonging to citizens of the United States as such, and not as citizens of a state". Wadleigh v. Newhall 136 F. 941 (1905)*

1. *"The government of the* **United States is a foreign corporation with respect to a state.**" *In re Merriam*, 36 N. E. 505, 141 N. Y. 479, affirmed 16 S. Ct. 1073, 163 U. S. 625, 41 L.Ed. 287.
2. *"The privileges and immunities of citizens of the United States, which are protected by the 14th Amendment, against abridgment by the states, are those which arise out of the essential nature and characteristics of the national government, the federal Constitution, treaties, or acts of Congress,* **as distinguished from those belonging to the Citizens of a state**; *Gardner v. Ray*, 157 S. W. 1147, 1150; *Hammer v. State*, 89 N. E. 850, 851, 173 Ind. 199, 24 L. R. A., N. S., 795, 140 Am. St. Rep. 248, 21 Ann. Cas. 1034.
3. *"On the other hand, there is a significant historical fact in all of this. Clearly, one of the purposes of the 13th and 14th Amendments and of the 1866 act and of section 1982* **was to give the Negro citizenship.** " *Jones v. Alfred H. Mayer Co.* (1967), 379 F.2d 33, 43.
4. *"It is true that the chief interest of the people in giving permanence and security to* **citizenship in the 14th Amendment was the desire to protect the Negroes.**" *Afroyim v. Rusk* (1967), 18 L.Ed. 2d 758, 764.

5. *"The object of the 14th Amendment, as is well known, was to confer upon the colored race the right of citizenship*." *United States v. Wong Kim Ark*, 169 U. S. 649, 692.

6. *"It would be a remarkable anomaly if the national government, without the amendment, could confer citizenship on aliens of every race or color, and citizenship, with civil and political rights, on the "inhabitants" of Louisiana and Florida, without reference to race or color, and cannot, with the help of the amendment, confer on those of the African race, who have been born and always lived within the United States, all that this law seeks to give them."* United States v. Rhodes (1866), 27 Fed. Cas. 785, 794.

7. *"The amendment referred to slavery. Consequently, the only persons embraced by its provisions, and for which Congress was authorized to legislate in the manner were those then in slavery."* Bowlin v. Commonwealth (1867), 65 Kent. Rep. 5, 29.

8. *"After the adoption of the 13th Amendment, a bill which became the first Civil Rights Act was introduced in the 39th Congress, the major purpose of which was to secure to the recently freed Negroes all the civil rights secured to white men. . . .(N)***one other than citizens of the United States were within the provisions of the Act.***"* *Hague v. C. I. O.*, 307 U. S. 496, 509.

9. **"No white person. . . owes the status of citizenship to the recent amendments to the Federal Constitution."** *Van Valkenbrg v. Brown* (1872), 43 Cal. Sup. Ct. 43, 47.

10. "The rights of the state, *as such, are not under consideration in the 14th Amendment, and* **are fully guaranteed by other provisions**." *United States v. Anthony* (1873), 24 Fed. Cas. 829 (No. 14,459), 830.

I think these are an astonishing group of decisions, in that they show just how prejudiced both Judges and many politicians were during this period. I found reading them unconscionable and disgraceful but enlightening in so far as the truth behind some legislation and in this case the 14th Amendment to the U.S. Constitution. Once a darker skinned person of African descent became free, having been here for generations, would they not just automatically become Citizens of their respective States?

Many contend that these decisions and the 14th Amendment itself, was to usher African Americans into Federal Citizenship, hence under the specific jurisdiction of the District of Columbia and not the 50 States. Consider that when Congress is legislating for the District of Columbia, it is not bound by the same constitutional limitations as when it is legislating for the 50 States. Has our entire citizenry been scammed by force and coercion into becoming Federal Citizens, hence liable for the Federal Individual Income Tax, the #9 definition of the various jurisdictions found within the Internal Revenue Code and why those living and working within Washington, DC pay both a state/District of Columbia Income Tax and a Federal Income Tax?

"An Unlimited Power to Tax, involves, necessarily, a Power to destroy" 17 U.S. 327

Although many believe the quote above by Supreme Court Justice John Marshall, 193 years ago, during the case *McCulloch* v. *Maryland*, was extremely important, in this authors opinion, the "ideological" truth emphasized, is far more importance. For that to be understood, the context of the case is important.

One of the two issues within the case, was about a State's "Right" to impose a tax on the Bank of the United States, our 1st central bank, later disbanded.

A central bank is the 5th platform within The Communist Manifesto, written by Karl Marx and Richard Engels, and what has now been reenacted and adopted in 1913, as the Federal Reserve Bank of the United States. The other issue was if Congress had the right to establish a central bank in the first place. I think the decision was wrong on both counts but that is another issue. In the case Justice Marshall went on to opine:

> *"That the power of taxing it [the bank] by the States may be exercised so as to destroy it, is too obvious to be denied, and That the power to tax involves the power to destroy [is] not to be denied."*

Philosophically, if a state or country can tax a central bank out of existence. Is it not possible for the State or Country to tax its Citizens, perhaps not out of existence, but surely into poverty?

We have in this country some 115 or so different taxes and regulatory fees incorporated into our local, state and Federal tax and regulatory systems.

Over 4,500 factories have closed down in the last 15 years alone. Our bankruptcy and foreclosure rates are at all-time highs. Our actual crime rates, according to court records, are being manipulated by law enforcement by underreporting criminal incidents and yet we still have the highest incarceration rates in the world. As government has grown and taxation increased, we have gone from the largest creditor nation in the world in 1900 to the largest debtor nation in the world today.

When you include all local, state and federal taxes and regulatory fees, we have one of the highest overall individual and corporate tax rates in the world, taking into consideration allowable deductions. We need to abolish both the income tax and the central bank.

CHAPTER 7
WINNERS AND LOSERS AGAINST THE IRS

There are those that have been lucky, and I use the term lucky for a reason in the matter of IRS collection activities. Most of these people, I'm told, all made the basic assertion and/or defense that there is no Federal Statute that requires Citizens of the 50 States to file and pay a Federal Individual Income Tax and that the government must show them the law. Of course, as you've read, this appears to be something no one in government appears willing to do. The luck, if you are able to get it, is a Judge that is not corrupt, competent council that is fearless because of IRS retaliations and a Jury that is smart enough to understand and weigh the issues.

There was Thomas Reeves of Paducah, KY who was **acquitted** by a jury in 1988; Franklin Sanders and (16) co-defendants in Memphis were **acquitted** in 1991; Gabriel Scott of Fairbanks, AK was **acquitted** in 1992; Lloyd Long of Chattanooga, TN was **acquitted** in 1993; Frederick Allnutt Sr. and his son Christopher Allnut of Baltimore, MD were **acquitted in Federal Court** on Criminal Charges (Fracke, 1996) in 1996; Gaylon Harrell of Logan County, IL was **acquitted** in 2000; Donald Fecay of Detroit, MI was **acquitted** in 2001; Vernice Kuglin of Memphis, TN was **acquitted** 2003; Dr. Lois Somerville of Lake Mary, FL was **acquitted** in 2003; Former IRS Special Agent Joe Banister was **acquitted** in 2005; Attorney Thomas Cryer of Shreveport, LA was **acquitted** in 2007; and American Airline pilot John Cheek of Illinois *Cheek v. United States*, 498 U.S. 192 (1991), was a US Supreme Court case where the Court reversed the conviction of John Cheek, for willful failure to file tax returns and tax evasion. There are many more winners but they're hard to find because of media bias on reporting and the lack of publishing cases in Circuit Courts.

As we've seen from the assortment of evidence provided, the government has thus far refused to provide the legislative Act, the Federal Statute that requires most State Citizens to both file and pay a Federal Individual Income Tax. There however is a long list of losers as well. The income tax issues are complex and hard to present, especially if Judges and Prosecutors are in cahoots to thwart an open and honest process. Once such case is noted below, but first some of the losers.

Some of the losers are Leona Helmsly, Wesley Snipes, Larkin Rose, Sherry Jackson; a former IRS agent, Ted McAnlis, Eddie Kahn, Doug Rosile, Irvin Schiff, and even Peter Hendrickson, author of Cracking The Code: the fascinating truth about taxation in America, just to name a few. Hendrickson obviously didn't Crack the Corruption.

Attorney Tommy Cryer, one of the winners, told one of my friends, the only reason he thought he had won his case is because he had an Attorney on his jury and that he thought this individual was able to assist the other jurors in understanding the important issues. Sadly the IRS and government corruption continues despite the various winners against them.

The case of Richard Simkanin stands out as an example of the corruption within the Federal Administration, a/k/a Federal Prosecutors at the Department of Justice and "especially" the Judiciary.

From Bedford, Texas, Simkanin was a part of the Tax Honesty Movement and a part of the We The People Foundation lawsuit against the government. He owned a small company and had his employees agree to not have their taxes withheld by his company on their behalf. The government tried to get two separate grand juries to indict in 2001 and 2002 and finally after the DOJ prevented Simkanin from appearing and testifying, they were able to get a third Grand Jury to indict. They did the same exact thing to John Ellis, Jeff Pollard, and Bob Koch in another suit of a similar nature, before getting the third grand jury to indict because they disallowed them from testifying at their own hearings.

Simkanin was tried soon after. Judge John McBryde, after having a jury deliberate for eight hours, sending out nine notes asking questions, declared a mistrial (Johnson, 2003) in Aug 2003.

Since withholding is one of the most substantial means for the government to enforce and collect the Federal Individual Income Tax, our corrupt government could not allow this to go unchallenged, despite what the laws says, or more importantly does not say. As a side note. Getting employers to withhold taxes on behalf of their employees is a holdover from the Victory Tax during WWII which was, as we've already shown, repealed two years later and didn't even apply to Citizens of the 50 States. People did it voluntarily to assist the war effort. Interestingly, it was the military contractors profiting from the war who were the biggest advocates and participants for collecting taxes from their employees. The government was running out of money so they enacted the Victory tax.

No one in the Tax Honesty movement knows the back room deals between the Judges and the powers to be, but the actions of the IRS, DOJ and Judges all the way up to the Supreme Court, gives us a clue, especially the We the People and Simkanin cases.

Simkanin had two attorneys, Arch McColl III and Doug Coffin. Both attorneys were well versed in "tax honesty" trials and McColl personally led the judicial investigation of Judge McBryde for judicial misconduct that resulted in McBryde's suspension from the bench and a call for his resignation in 1999. Coffin said he was prepared to lose his bar license defending Simkanin's beliefs and to insure justice is done. Like I said, fearless.

Although Simkanin, had no prior arrest record, he was still held in jail after the mistrial was declared. The Judge had not provided the information that the Jury had requested of the government, creating a tenuous situation that prompted Judge McBride, obviously an extremely biased Judge in favor of the government and the Income Tax, to call a mistrial instead of allowing the jury to find Simkanin "not" guilty. Since the Prosecution was obviously unable to provide the answers to what the Jurors had requested, the Judge knew by the questions, that this jury understood the issues and the inability to provide the Federal Statue was obviously one of those questions. The mistrial allowed a retrial and thus the Judge could keep Simkanin in custody on the erroneous allegation that he had made threats to kill federal Judges. His Attorney, Arch McColl said that it was a disbarred attorney that had made the fabricated accusation. Obviously, a den of thieves, a disbarred attorney and a suspended Judge, complicit in a conspiracy to deprive the rights of Citizens. One can only imagine what went on behind the scenes to get to these unscrupulous parties to do what they did.

A mistrial is supposed to be granted when something happens or someone says something that causes some unfairness and thus one of the parties, from not receiving a fair trial. A mistrial is not supposed to be granted just because the Defendant in this case appears like they may win.

They needed to prosecute Simkanin or the news would quickly get out and spread like wildfire, prompting others to stop withholding on behalf of their employees. Interestingly, ex-IRS Special Agent Joe Banister had helped Simkanin with going through the process of getting his employees to agree in writing to not withhold their taxes, which they all agreed to. Bannister was also indicted and tried, but was much luckier and was acquit-

ted by his jury. The suit against Bannister, was obviously retaliation for his vocal opposition and activities for being in the tax
honest movement and part of the We The People v. United States
suit. Ex-IRS Agent Sherry Jackson, also a member of the We the
People Foundation, who is just as vocal wasn't so lucky. Both are
great patriots and despite Joe being prosecuted and Sherry going
to prison, they continue their teachings of what those in the movement believe is the truth. Fearless in my opinion.

Judge McBryde understood the potential ramifications
and obviously knew the Government was going to try to indict
and prosecute Simkanin again. They did, and this time with significant evidence disallowed by the Judge, they were able to get
the jury to convict. I'm told the level of corruption and collusion
that went on in the second trial could make a book just on its own.
Arch McColl, the Dallas lawyer representing Simkanin, said his
client was denied a fair trial because the judge, McBryde did not
allow him to present key evidence on whether Social Security,
Medicare and income taxes are voluntary. It is one thing to keep
the money of those who you are withholding for and not pay the
government. That would be what is called unjust enrichment. It is
another thing to be prosecuted for owing money to the government for someone else that you did not get the money from, which
was the basis of Simkanin's case. He did go back and try to get
for his employees, the previous money that he had paid to the IRS
on their behalf. They prosecuted him for making fraudulent returns on this issue.

No "law" or IRS code demanding most employers to withhold taxes was identified in either trial. When Simkanin's attorney
Arch McColl attempted to query government witnesses about the
legal definition of "wages," Texas Star-Telegram reporter Max
Baker wrote that Judge McBryde "told the jurors they could not
question the constitutionality of the tax code."

Richard Simkanin, died while he was in Federal Prison, as a "real" political prisoner. God rest his soul for his courage. After spending 7 years in prison, Simkanin missed a probation appointment with his parole officer and was sentenced by Judge McBryde for seven (7) additional years. This should sicken and outrage most people. Judge McBryde obviously wanted to scare the hell out of anyone who would attempt what Simkanin did. As with almost all Federal Indictments under Title 26, Simkanin's indictment failed to cite any of the specific Federal Statutes that imposed a legal duty on him to withhold income taxes from his employees. (Note: virtually all federal tax "crime" indictments, Title 26 USC 7203, "Willful Failure to File" apply to various Internal Revenue taxes and no Federal Statute is ever provided by the US DOJ that specifically requires Citizens of the 50 States to file and pay a Federal Individual Income tax much less withhold them by an employer.) The John Cheek case should have stopped the prosecution for Willful Failure to File; a continuance of corruption.

Title 26, as we have seen, is not Positive Law according to the U.S. House of Representative's own Office of the Law Revision Counsel and therefore it should not be used in any courtroom. Surely it should not be used in an indictment and/or complaint. The IRS will try to utilize Title 26 in its lawsuits because of the complexities of our laws. We've seen that there are at least nine (9) different jurisdictions defining State(s) and/or the "United States" in Title 26, thus making it hard to know which laws are subject to which jurisdictional limitations. If you add in the Citizenship issue, it muddies the waters even more.

As I mentioned the Internal Revenue Code (IRC) is a compilation of all the Tax laws enacted by Congress since the inception of the Constitution and different Sections apply to different jurisdictions. At trials, they start throwing around Code Sections as if they all apply to the Federal Individual Income Tax when in fact only as small Section of the IRC applies to this and the jurisdiction is very specific as we have seen. Internal appears to be very specific and that is of the District of Columbia, which would thus be "Internal" to the Federal Government. The Internal Revenue Code is a set of laws applying to the internal working of the Federal Government. As noted above, they do not have taxing authority over Citizens of the 50 United States, except in specific situation. I understand this is the short version and the arguments are as confusing as the jurisdictions I presented. I've always thought that it was written this way and put together in the manner so it would be difficult to analysis and defend.

We have an entire body of law that is **"not"** considered "Positive" Law, that was enacted by Congress on three (3) separate occasions; the Internal Revenue Code of _____ 1939, 1954 & 1986, as a single piece of legislation. Why would they need to enact the entire IRC when all the laws in the IRC have allegedly already been enacted?

CHAPTER 8
ARGUMENTS AGAINST THIS ANALYSIS

The 16ᵗʰ Amendment

Some claim that the 16th Amendment to the Constitution in 1913, plays a role in the enforcement of taxation of the Citizens of the 50 States. Let us assume that the 16th Amendment to the Constitution did give the Congress the right to enact a direct income tax on Citizens in a private capacity, even though there are judicial decisions and evidence to the contrary.

Congress, as you now know, must still pass a law (a Federal Statute) that provides all the specifics that would apply to the Tax. Congress must still create a law that tells the Citizens who, what, when, how much, to whom and where to pay the tax.

Pollock v. Farmers' Loan and Trust Co., 157 U.S. 429 (1894), 158 U.S. 601 (1895). In this case even though the Supreme Court of the United States (SCOTUS) noted that the 16th Amendment conferred no new powers of taxation, some conclude that the income tax was constitutional because Congress always had the power to lay and collect taxes, it was just that it required apportionment, which the 16th Amendment now provides. There are even some issues as to if the 16th Amendment was legally ratified, but you would have to read the book The Law That Never Was by William Benson and Red Beckman to see for yourself. I myself have read their book and agree to their premise.

Let's assume that Congress has the power to lay and collect a direct tax on income as some suggest. The problem with this position is as noted above. Congress must still enact a law that would become a Federal Statute that tells the Citizens of the 50 States, who, what, when, how much, to whom and where to pay the tax. Show us that Law!

The Burden of Proof still lies upon the various Officers and Officials of the Federal Government of the United States to provide to the Citizens the Statute, the date it was signed into law and to answer the 62 questions posed in the formal Redress of Grievance provided by the "We the People Foundation" on the issue of Federal Individual Income Taxation, as required by the 1st Amendment to the Constitution.

Doesn't it seem a bit odd to <u>have the 1st Amendment in our Constitution, if the Government does not have to answer our questions in a formally submitted petition?</u> I learned many years ago to always question authority.

The Income Tax Act of 1913
& the Victory Tax of 1942

Some suggest that the **Income Tax Act of 1913** began the direct tax on Individual Income. However, if this was true, **why** would President Franklin D. Roosevelt's New Deal programs necessitate Congress to enact **The Revenue Act of 1935**, introducing a Wealth Tax, a new progressive tax that took up to 75 percent of the highest incomes to help pay for his programs? Most American's never met the necessary income levels of the Income Tax Act of 1913, thus there was, as some suggest, already a tax on the highest income earners in place. Why pass another income tax if one was already in place; just amend it.

Additionally, if there was already an individual income tax Act in effect, why would there be a need to enact the **Revenue Act of 1937**, revising the 1935 Act? Again, why didn't they just amend the Income Tax Act of 1913?

Now here's the most interesting observation in my opinion. The cost of World War II was exceeding federal revenues so much that Congress enacted **The Revenue Act of 1942**, nick named the **Victory Tax**, supposedly the broadest and most progressive tax in American history. The government even helped to ease the taxpayer's burden of paying a lump sum from this tax, and to create a regular flow of revenue into the Treasury, the government required employers to withhold money from employee's paychecks. Does this procedure of withholding sound familiar? By the end of the war in 1945, about 90 percent of American workers submitted income tax forms. OK, so let assume this law is when the Federal Individual Income Tax was actually enacted that still lasts through today. Not so fast, the Victory Tax was repealed in 1944.

[Act May 29, 1944, 7 p. m., E. W. T., c. 210, 58 Stat. 234.]
SEC   6.   REPEAL   OF   VICTORY   TAX
(a) In general. Subchapter D of Chapter 1 (relating to the victory tax) is repealed.

Many just assume that these various acts placed a burden upon the citizens of the 50 States. The Victory Tax was actually a voluntary tax for most Americans as it was a tax as per IRC Sec. 211, a tax on nonresident alien individuals, but as part of the war effort many State Citizens participated out of patriotism to help win the war. In my opinion this is the enactment, although repealed, that our government continues to erroneously enforce today. Once again, why enact the victory tax if you could just amend a prior income tax such as the 1913 or 1935 Acts, if one was already in existence? The answer was obvious; there wasn't one or they would not have enacted the victory tax and they would have just amended the prior tax and nicknamed it the Victory Tax.

From the website Constitutional Society at http://www.constitution.org/tax/us-ic/hist/victorytax.htm:`` "Prior to World War II, no one outside the government paid an income tax; the people were, and understood themselves to be, immune from that tax. During WWII, Congress passed the Victory Tax (56 stat. 884) to impose an income tax on every individual in the United States of America, something which had not been done by any previous income tax act. Excepted from that tax were those already paying income taxes per IRC Sec. 211 - nonresident alien individuals with no United States business or office but living in a "contiguous country" and having income from United States sources."

It is quite clear that no personal income tax on Citizens of the 50 States existed up until 1942 and "The Revenue Act of 1942" did not impose a tax on this group either. Citizens of the 50 States participated in the tax voluntarily out of patriotism.

The 16th Amendment did not provide any new taxing authority and congress cannot constitutionally enact a law that takes away the property rights of the Citizens of the 50 States. The money we trade in exchange for our labor is our property and it cannot be taxed according to 200 plus years of case law. The exception being unless that individual falls within the jurisdiction of the federal government through either a privileged occupation such as a federal official or a product or service that is specifically regulated by the Federal government.

As an IRS agent told a good friend, "you may be right Mr. X, but that's not how the game is played."

CHAPTER 9
NOTICE AND CASE FOR FRAUD AND TREASON

There is no more pressing an issue to the welfare of our great nation than the constitutional protections of unalienable rights being usurped and the various abrogations of our Bill of Rights, two of which have been shown in this book. Sadly, there are numerous more, but these are enough to show that our government and Rule of Law has been hijacked by nefarious means, some naïve and some complicit throughout our history.

The erroneous Notices of Federal Tax Liens and their **fraudulent enforcement by those within the Federal Government and Judiciary, are inconsistent to Amendment V. - No person shall….. be deprived of life, liberty or property without due process of law**. The government will not nor has not shown the Citizens of the 50 United States the specific Federal Statute they are enforcing. Most of the enforcement does not fall under the purview of due process as does all other aspects of our rule of law. The IRS and Treasury seem to be the only entities in the United States immune from following the rule of law as everyone else must do.

The "Right" as protected by the 1st Amendment to petition the Government for Redress of Grievances has been ignored by various members of our **Judiciary because they** will not force these Federal Officials, to specify the Federal Statute or statutes they are enforcing and answer the various questions posed in the Petition and thus appear to be **complicit in the abrogation of the 1st Amendment and the fraudulent enforcement of a Federal Individual Income Tax.**

What those within the tax honesty movement have found over the years is that, because of the complexity, many individuals within the IRS and government are naïve as to the erroneous Kind of Tax being used to do the assessments, Notices of Federal Tax Liens and enforcement of a Federal Individual Income Tax against Citizens of the United States of America. This presents a valid rationale for its continued enforcement by those that are naïve to the issues. Jobs are surely scarce and no one can belittle another for doing a job, even if it is the most loathsome job on the planet; that of a tax collector.

However, some like ex-IRS Special Agent Joe Bannister, Sherry Jackson who was an ex-forensic accountant for the IRS, and John Turner, an ex-collection Agent in California have all joined the Tax Honesty Movement.

With this book as additional evidence, naivety can no longer be used as a rationale for the continued enforcement until such time as the corrections are made as to the Kind of Tax being assessed and noted on the NFTLs used to start the actually collection process.

Please understand that I may not have every single issue I have written about perfectly analyzed and properly represented in this book. However my overall conclusions are self-evident to anyone who reads the laws and information I have provided. I'm a Realtor and Real Estate consultant and everything that I have done and all the knowledge that I have acquired over the years has been on a part time basis. Obviously, if someone like myself doesn't expose the truth, we cannot rely on those who benefit from the system, like tax Attorneys, CPAs and other tax return preparers or the Judges to expose it. It's taken me close to two years just to determine an outline and write this book. As an example, I do not actually know when the actual enforcement of the tax starts. It does not appear to really start with the Notice of Federal Tax Lien, yet they will take peoples wages and money from their bank accounts once the NFTL is filed. I don't really understand why they can do this without a Court Order. Remember, I'm not an Attorney, so I can only rely on what I and others have observed and experienced. It appears to be just a Notice. As an example, one of my associates was served by process and taken to Federal Court to collect what they alleged he owed. He had a home with equity in it so the IRS took him to court to get a court order to sell his house and take his money, based on the NFTL. Based on the above situation it could be argued that the actual collection really must be started by a legal suit and adjudicated by a court order.

However, this analysis is really moot because the NFTL itself is still be fraudulent. Here is what the NFTL does note;
"As provided in sections 6321, 6322, and 6323, of the Internal Revenue Code, notice is given that taxes (including interest and penalties) have been assessed against the following named taxpayer. Demand is for payment of the liability has been made, but it remains unpaid. Therefore there is a lien in favor of the United States on all property and rights to property belonging to this taxpayer for the amount of the taxes, and additional penalties, interest, and cost that may accrue."

As a reminder, 6321, 6322 and 6323 all are part of the Chapter 64.–COLLECTION.

Because of this disclosure on the NFTL, Title Companies will "not" provide title insurance on real property that is transferred unless the existing NFTL(s) are removed for the Public Records or satisfies under IRS guidelines. All the Attorneys we spoke with on this subject believe it to be a valid lien and thus tell us it transfers with the property. The courts appear to side with this belief but I don't know if the evidence I provide has yet been used in a court case. If the notice is defective as I have shown, how could it be enforceable?

On the same subject another legal researcher sued the IRS for Quite Title, a State court issue, to try to eliminate the NFTL that was filed against his wife and the IRS had the case moved to Federal Court. The US Attorney then moved to dismiss the case on lack of subject matter jurisdiction and was granted his motion. The same thing happens to one of my very close friends. He filed a petition for quite title in Circuit Court, a state action according to everything I know and immediately the Defendant, the USA put in a motion to move the case to Federal Court. At the same time the Federal Court then asked for a dismissal based on lack of subject matter jurisdiction. Two cases with the same results.

I point these two cases out to show the games the judicial system can play if they want to defeat you, caring little about justice or the law. You even have to be cognizant of the ethos of the Lawyer you hire, because he could be a party/cronies of the team, making sure you lose. There are many other stories on the numerous strategies the government uses to win, but there are sufficient books already on the subject, so there is little need to go any further. It's so bad that even many of the lawyers are constantly complaining about it. Just like in the political arena, there are two basic sides fighting over the power to control the courts. This is one of the reasons why the Governorships and Judicial nominations are so important to the two sides. The Governors in most States nominate Judges just like the President does. Not only that, they move the Judges around depending on who they want hearing which cases. You can find this by researching the Governor of your State's Executive Orders they has signed.

These type actions by the judiciary do not diminish their complicity, when they knowingly are involved in the current fraud. However, those that have been previously appraised of the evidence and ignored the evidence as well as were involved in the defeat of the Petition for Redress of Grievances are in defiance of our Constitution and their Oaths of Office.

On the other hand, when I read some of the court decisions, some of the decisions are correct. Individuals made claim, what the IRS and Courts call Frivolous Claims. If a Judge hears one of these type claims, they have no choice but to rule in the government's favor.

You have now been provided both material and substantive amounts of circumstantial evidence that shows the so-called Federal Individual Income Tax is being erroneously enforced by various individuals within a number of Agencies in the Federal Administration and the Judiciary. If they continue to participate in its enforcement, given this evidence, they are now complicit in this fraudulent activity against various Citizens and our Constitution, by deliberate fraud, malicious prosecution and theft. Thusly, they are abrogating the United States Constitution and usurping the property rights of millions of Citizens.

Logically, for any lien to be valid, it must have proper evidence of its authority and jurisdiction noted on it. If not, any government agency of anyone else could just file a lien or levy against someone and literally fabricate their authority and jurisdiction if the evidence for their authority and jurisdiction are not required as part of any enforcement action. As you now understand, you can no longer even "ask" questions relating to the tax and expect them to be answered. If a government agency can tax or fine on a whim, then there is no rule of law nor do our unalienable rights any longer exist. Therefore, our founding fathers and all those who have fought for our liberties after them, have risked their lives, liberty and fortunes for naught and We the People have been economically shackled by devious people under a guise of the rule of law and justice.

When one or more individuals are "knowingly" involved in a fraudulent scheme and thus an illegal act, it becomes a conspiracy. When the rule of law, the foundation of any constituted republic is unlawfully abrogated, thus usurping the rights and property of Citizens, it is an insurrection and thus a treasonous act punishable as such.

Those enforcing the Federal Individual Income Tax have "not" shown the Citizens the law and have used nefarious and unlawful means to enforce the confiscation of property and continue to do so. They will not even note the correct Kind of Tax being enforced on their various correspondences, notices, liens and administrative levies.

They have refused to answer questions posed by constitutional scholars, tax Attorneys and other learned individuals provided to them multiple times in a Formal Redress of Grievances as guaranteed by our Constitution. They have denied reasonable due process to millions of Citizens of our great nation over long periods of time. The Supreme Court of the United States even refused to hear the case involving our 1st Amendment right to have our grievances redressed by simply forcing those administering and enforcing a so-called law to answer relevant questions relating to the various tax laws, their enforcement, authority and jurisdiction.

Those involved in this conspiracy to unjustly enrich themselves and others within the bureaucracy through the unjust enforcement of a Federal Individual income tax are committing treason if they cannot provide a Federal Statute that grants them authority and jurisdiction.

If you are involved in any way with the unlawful collection of the 1040, 941 or any other erroneous Kind or Type of Tax on a Notice of Federal Tax Lien or any other erroneous tax collections under Title 26; Internal Revenue Code that has NOT been enacted into Federal Statue, you are hereby given notice that if you continue to be involved in the unlawful collection of these taxes, you will, or at least you should be deemed a co-conspirator in one or more of the following; fraud, theft, slander, libel, unjust enrichment, malicious prosecution, perjury and other potential crimes associated with the unlawful confiscation and theft of money and property from the Citizens of the United States of America.

Those that have been and continue to be involved in both the fraud and co-conspiratorial conduct to create this enforcement that continues the theft, slander and unjust enrichment using the unlawful collection of taxes are guilty of potentially several crimes. Like many Judges who are condoning these activities through Judicial prejudice and corruption, these individuals are operating in a direct conflict and defiance of our rule of law.

We however, cannot necessarily justly penalize those that are held impotent and captive by the confiscatory and retaliatory nature of government. We have seen what the system does to whistleblowers and those that challenge government force and co-ercion.

Do not conclude however my disdain and contempt for their actions, but just stopping the continued actions of the fraud-ulent enforcement will suffice in accomplishing the goals of tak-ing our great nation into the 21st century with greater liberty and prosperity. The Federal Income Tax needs to be stopped now and forever. In a nation whose rule of law is based on liberty, an indi-vidual's labor and justly acquired property is their life and it should remain free from the grasps of government so that all hu-man beings may pursue their highest goals and potential achieve-ments.

I therefore ask you to provide this book to individuals such as CPAs, Tax Attorneys, The County Clerks, management within companies that provide tax filing services such as H&R Block and Liberty Tax Services, all Attorneys, Judges, Title Insurance Com-panies and all businesses that are participating in some way in the obvious and erroneous collection of Federal Individual Income taxes and to show them the fraud being perpetrated upon its citizens.

Purpose and Intent of the Notices

Sitting by and letting others take the risk, because you are afraid to blow the whistle in this day and age is now an erroneous emotion. Those in positions of power have too many others who are now exposing their unjust and unlawful actions. We must join people such as Julian Assange of Wikileaks who has exposed Federal government corruption, Edward Snowden who has exposed the NSA's unlawful surveillance and Karen Hughes, a graduate of Yale Law School that has exposed the central banking oligarchs, after 20 years of experience in the legal department at the World Bank.

The following Notice and Affidavit was prepared by myself, without the assistance of any attorney and should be considered as such. It should be rewritten by a competent Attorney to reflect the actual number of NFTL(s) that have been filed against you and should be addressed and sent, along with this book to all those individuals who have sent you any IRS notices or correspondence, as well as to the local Clerk of Court where the NFTL(s) are filed.

The affidavit should attest to the truth as it relates to your specific Notice of Federal Tax Liens and correspondences. This makes it impossible to write a single notice that fits all possible Notices and Affidavits.

You should seek competent council to prepare the various notice(s) and affidavit(s) to the appropriate individuals and if someone is able to have the various notices prepared, please share them with the rest of the Citizens of this country. Your Congresspersons, State Representatives and even the President of the United States should to be notified by the thousands. Perhaps it will sink in if they receive enough of them. This is an important part of the re-establishment of our rule of law.

Notice to the Proper Authorities

Please be advised that the Kind of Tax, column (a) noted on the attached Notice of Federal Tax Lien(s) (NFTL)#_____ recorded in OR Book _____ /Page _____ in _____ County, _____ is/are erroneous and therefore insufficient as a valid lien. See Exhibits A1 & A2.

After having reviewed the evidence within the NFTL(s) noted above, as the Named Individual on the NFTL(s), as per the following attached Affidavit, see Exhibit B, I, _____acknowledge and affirmed, to the best of my belief and ability, that the Kind of Tax(s) noted on the NFTL(s) is/are incorrect, that the named individual does not owe the erroneous Kind of Tax noted on the NFTL and therefore the NFTL(s) is/are insufficient as a lien(s) because they lack proper notification as to the authority and jurisdiction affected.

As evidence, the attached book, The Achilles Heel; the IRS Notice of Federal Tax Lien is hereby provided to show that the erroneous Kind of Tax(s), on the above noted Notice of Federal Tax Lien(s) is incorrect. The attached NFTL(s) shown in Exhibits A1 & A2 are insufficient and therefore must be removed because they are invalid and therefore unlawful liens.

Failure to remove, rescind, withdraw or correct these insufficient and therefore defective NFTL(s), after being provided this Official Notification and the following evidence, allows those that created this erroneous lien(s) to continue their slander against me, causing detrimental harm to my life, liberty and property. It also diminishes my credit score and ratings, diminishes my borrowing capabilities, usurps my constitutional rights and allows for the continued fraudulent enforcement of the taking of money and property in an unlawful scheme against me and other Citizens of the United States of America.

Affidavit for Notice

TO: _____

    Named REVENUE OFFICER as noted on Form 668(Y)(c) Department of the Treasury, Internal Revenue Service _____(see addendum for the various address(s))

_____ sent via Certified Return Receipt # _____

    Please be advised that the Notice of Federal Tax Lien (Notice) issued by the Department of the Treasury – Internal Revenue Service on Form 668 (Y)(c) dated ___(Date)_____ and filed at the ___Name of County Court House_____ at ___OR Book and Page___ to ____Name of Taxpayer, notes the incorrect Kind of Tax in column (a).

    I, _____ hereby affirm under penalty of perjury of the United States of America that I have not received, during the "Tax Periods Ending" as noted in column (b) of the attached Notice, Exhibit A, any Income as noted under Title 26, Section _Numerical Kind of Tax 1040, 941, 1020 etc.,_ Internal Revenue Code, as the NFTL notes in column (a). I am not aware of owing any tax of that kind "_____" as notated on the above filed Notice of Federal Tax Lien and therefore would like to place on Notice both the Individual or individuals who made the assessment and who issued the Notice or Notices (see above), of this fact.

Please make the necessary arrangements to either correct the "Kind of Tax" in column (a) on my NFTL or have the NFTL(s) immediately withdrawn.

Failure to do so in a timely manner as prescribed by various Federal and State laws will indicate that such actions, if not corrected and/or completed, are condoned by the named individual or individuals above and by the various Officers and Officials of the Department of the Treasury Internal Revenue Service.

(Affidavits *must* be notarized)

CHAPTER 10
ADDITIONAL COMMENTS

The key to any significant change has always been knowledge and this is why it is so important to officially notice everyone that is currently involved in the assessment and collection of the Federal Individual Income Tax, including the Clerks of Court and even CPAs and other tax return preparers.

Simply put, once someone has been formally noticed of their involvement in any fraudulent scheme and thus criminal activity in their daily job functions and responsibilities, they then become liable "individually". If they are involved with others such as in a business or other government entities, they also become a co-conspirators in the fraud. If they don't know that they are doing something fraudulent or criminally wrong, especially as difficult as the components of the issue are, there may not be malice or criminal intent on their part. Giving someone proper "Notice" changes that, because they now have been clearly shown the material and circumstantial evidence. They cannot claim ignorance or just doing their assigned job as they now know they are complicit in the fraud.

So now that you clearly understand the fraud involved, it behooves everyone in this great country of ours to inform every IRS agent, Judge and everyone else involved in continuing this horrendous confiscation of wealth from the Citizens of the United States, by showing this book as evidence.

If you are having any doubts as to the social ramification of this, please just ask yourself why are there so many people struggling economically today in this country. In the last published count, 48.8 million people were on food stamps alone and 1/3 or approximately 100 million people are living at or near the poverty line. Isn't it time to stop the socialistic/communistic trending in this country? I believe judicial and not political activism is the key to addressing and solving this injustice. Abolishing the fraudulent collection of the Federal Individual Income Tax would be one huge step.

The case for fraud, treason and insurrection is subject to those involved having the specific knowledge and understanding of their actions, as it relates to the actual erroneous assessments, the issuance of erroneous Notice of Federal Tax Lien(s) and collection activities. I would submit that very few people understand the various elements of the erroneous activities involved and thus, like most, are ignorant to the deceptions being fostered by those that do know, have known or who actually were involved in creating the system. That is why it is so important to get this information out.

Those involved in the Prosecution of Citizens within the IRS and the Department of Justice and those hearing the various cases, such as those Federal Judges, including those Supreme Court Judges who refused to hear the case, who were involved in the blatant abrogation of the Constitution, as we have observed in the We The People v. United States, is another issue. There is substantive evidence of various "alleged" criminal activities by Judges and prosecutors throughout the enforcement process that have shown a disdain for our rule of law and Constitution. These people obviously know, and if they don't, they should. "Ignorance, especially at those levels, as they say, is no excuse". When individuals in positions of authority break the rule of law to favor those in power and those special interests, what then becomes of our rule of law?

We have already observed numerous Judges that are willing to break or ignore the rule of law. There are numerous stories, too many to disclose, of many other usurpations of rights during enforcement, such as, dismissing cases, issuance of fines for so-called frivolous claims, denying material evidence from being presented or just ignoring material evidence.

Additionally, erroneous claims by prosecutors and bad case decisions by corrupt Judges are a huge problem. Sadly, many of those who have tried to provide evidence have been fraudulently imprisoned by the various Judges and Justice Department prosecutors.

This book because of the material evidence provided, changes things, until such time as Government Officials are able or willing to provide the true Kind of Tax being enforced and note it correctly on the Notice of Federal Tax Lien.

We have exposed their Achilles Heel. Now it is time to sever it and cripple the system for life. More importantly, we must reestablish our liberties and individual rights that are guaranteed by the Constitution of the United States.

The various players are literally involved in a conspiracy to abrogate our rule of law, thus overthrowing our lawfully constituted democratic Republic. This action, by a relatively small group of people, by definition, appears to be treason and an insurrection against the Citizens and Government of the United States of America.

Let's assume, just for discussion purposes that they won't show us the statute, because they can't, otherwise they would have showed us long ago and provided such evidence.

As you have read, I have provided additional information on jurisdiction, Citizenship and other aspects of our law to attempt to lay out the case as to why our rights have been usurped. An income tax is very important to those in power. As previously noted government has a propensity to tax and this is why our nation has ended up with over 115 different forms of taxation enforced by the various levels of government.

What I am writing now is my opinion but it is also the opinion of many others such as Professor of Economics Thomas DiLorenzo of Loyola College in Maryland, from his bestselling book "The Real Lincoln; A new look at Abraham Lincoln, His Agenda and an Unnecessary War". The Civil War as we should now know, was waged over much more than just slavery and the cessation of the southern States. It was also about the political struggle over greater centralized power and taxation. The money interests with its accumulated wealth predominantly in the North East, still remained much intact despite many of them having been on the wrong side of the Revolutionary War. These money interests had long profited from taxation, funneling the money into such entities as the military industrial complex and infrastructure spending on railroads. Tariffs and subsidies to corporations for railroad expansion, just so happened to be another one of the not so written about issues behind the Civil War that by the way was primarily instigated by the Republican Party of Abraham Lincoln, of which he played a role as a land speculator on railroad stations subsidies by the Government he would eventual sign into law.

The same thing is still happening today and is why the US is almost always in a constant state of war somewhere in the world. The money collected from the Federal Personal Income Tax is used in part to fund the largest military industrial complex in the world, reported in 2013, larger then the next 11 countries combined spending according to IHS Jane's Annual Defense Budgets Review. http://press.ihs.com/press-release/aerospace-de-fense-terrorism/global-defence-budgets-overall-rise-first-time-five-years

The U.S. estimated Defense budget for 2014 is $600,400,000,000. That's $600 billion, 400 million dollars and your money, taken from you under a fraudulent collection scheme is making military contractors extremely wealthy off of warfare.

Just remember the old cliché; those who live by the sword die by the sword, and I'm noting our countries foreign policy. Those in power send the poor and middle class into harm's way. The days of even the military commanders leading their soldiers into war, is a thing of the past and why today they are mostly war hawks.

Since it appears that no law has ever been passed that requires Citizens of the 50 States to file and pay a Federal tax on their individual labor in an individual capacity, those in power needed to then deceive the general public into believing they owe such a tax, even abrogating the rule of law, when necessary.

Overview of Income Tax History

As previously mentioned, the Victory Tax during WWII gave the Federal Government the opportunity to not only get many Citizens to pay income taxes out of patriotism, but to also have the tax collected by employers, thus now being able to hold the employers liable if they did not collect the tax from their employees.

With hundreds of thousands of soldiers coming back from the WWII, people obviously weren't paying attention over the next decade or so to what was going on in Washington, because they were so focused on getting their lives back in order.

Military Contractors and other companies who began retooling for peacetime productivity, continued to enforce the Victory Tax, now being called and collected as the Federal Individual Income Tax with the enactment of the Internal Revenue Code of 1939, reenacted in 1954. Remember, that not only was the Victory tax repealed, but it was actually a tax just on Resident Aliens, so it did not apply to most Citizens.

The question is, did it apply to the United States Citizens (Black Americans) who were placed under Federal jurisdiction by the 14th Amendment. The Federal Judiciary "of course" ruled that it did, hence forcing millions of free African Americans into the Federal Individual Income Tax system even though such a law didn't any longer exist nor were Blacks really anymore Federal Citizens than whites. We are all State Citizens united under our Federal Government giving rise to being Citizens of the United States of America; as shown different from being United States Citizens. The latter should be abolished as it appears to give rise to lesser inalienable rights, because all rights for all Citizens should be protected equally under our Constitution. That however is the mastery of the Judiciary in action, arrogant folks who deem themselves able and more importantly competent to rule over others; exactly what the Bill of Rights was supposed to stop.

Interestingly, an Internal Revenue Law did exist during the Civil War, but it was inclusive to just the Federal conclave of the District of Columbia, forts, arsenals and territorial possessions hence the term "internal". Remember, DC is the military command center where our Commander and Chief resides and operates. That is where the Federal Official comes into play in the "performance of the functions of a public office" with Judges and even Attorneys being Officers of the Court. It can be argued that the Supreme Court and all of its subsidiaries such as State and County Courts are a function of the Federal Government described within the Constitution under Article III, hence why Judges lost a legal suit and became the first Federal Individual Income Tax taxpayers. For me, all income taxes both individual and corporate, whether State or Federal are horrible taxes because they tax our labor, either directly or indirectly. A Judge should not be taxed just because he is a Federal Official. Why tax production and the hard work of people when excise taxes such as sales taxes, import and export taxes are available? Apparently there is never enough money for our illustrious politicians to squander. They even start printing it if they run out, even though it debases and devalues our money.

Go back and review the appalling court cases on Citizenship and the 14th Amendment. It also gives us an insight into the quality of people our judiciary and legal system have offered. Remember that it has always been the Judiciary that rubber stamps the usurping of individual rights in every atrocity throughout history. From the Christian Crusades to the Salem Witch Hunts, Judges have always presided over enforcement and punishment.

No matter where you live in this country or what race you are, you have Unalienable Rights; rights that cannot be relinquished or transferred, period. Just as the Attorney in the gun control case in the District of Colombia noted, the Judge usurped the Rights of Citizens living in the District of Columbia, somehow concluding that they have less rights than those people living in the other 50 States. In some aspects, for those living and working in the District of Columbia, it is considered another State and Congress makes the laws for them, **"exclusive"** of the other 50 States. This is important, but a State has no greater ability to usurp a right than does the Federal Government over the District of Columbia. Because the Federal Government makes laws for our military and its operations headquartered in the District of Columbia, the Judiciary has erroneously concluded that Congress is therefore not always bound by the same Constitutional limitations, as when they are legislating for the 50 States. Another bad decision that has given rise to the invasion of numerous foreign countries without the constitutionally mandated Declarations of War. Not since WWII has there been a Declaration of War enacted by Congress.

***"In exercising this power [to dispose of and make all needed Rules and Regulations **respecting the Territory or other Property belonging to the United States**[2]], Congress is not subject to the same constitutional limitations, as when*

it is legislating for the United States³. [Hooven & Allison Co. vs Evatt, 324 U.S. 652 (1945)]"

In this case the **United States² means the District of Columbia, all forts and arsenals, and other territorial possessions. Whereas in general, the United States³ means the 50 States, DC, forts, ports and arsenals, Puerto Rico, all territorial possession and the continental waters and bay bottom. Review, if necessary the 9 <u>different</u> definitions of the terms "States" and "United States" in the Internal Revenue Code to see all the jurisdictions.

Basically, my understanding of the intention of the separation of powers between the Federal conclave, the District of Columbia and the 50 United States, was for military purposes and operations. We have seen that those Presidents who declare a State of Emergency, thus become in a sense military dictators as both Abraham Lincoln and Franklin Roosevelt did. Lincoln, before and during the war, under a State of Emergency, suspended Habeas Corpus and arrested many people, even in the northern States who were in opposition of his policies. He closed down northern newspapers and even arrested a Federal Judge from a northern State, who was deemed a southern sympathizer for speaking out against Lincoln and the Republicans.

FDR confiscated, under Executive Order 6102 in 1933, all non-numismatic gold from those people stupid enough to turn it in under a so-called State of Emergency, he himself declared. The paper currency that was issued to those people who did turn in their gold, within weeks, again by his executive order, was then worth about 40% less than the value of the actual gold they were forced to turn in. FDR actually set the price of gold higher than what his Administration had paid the Citizens for it.

These type actions are not supposed to occur in our democratic republic of the United States because of specifically the Bill of Rights and the protective clauses of our Constitution. It doesn't matter what you believe, there are specific lawful methods of altering the law, and especially our Federal Government has not followed them. This has in turn, given rise for the State and local governments to follow suit in various manners to usurp their Citizens state rights. After the Civil War, many of the States, like Florida were forced to completely rewrite and pass new State Constitutions. The people within the Confederacy were forced out of their political positions in favor of those who were advocates of greater centralized power.

I'll concede that Lincoln was smart enough to emancipate the slaves, but it was not because he and his Republicans wanted racial equality. They wanted greater centralized power and the abolition of slavery was the tradeoff, what we call political compromise today. Remember Lincoln's Republican Party was responsible for enacted the Fugitive Slave laws that were sending slaves back from especially the northeast to their southern owners. Not only that, according to another one of DiLorenzo's books "Lincoln Unmasked", he provides evidence that Lincoln was a white separatist, wanting to actually exile all freed blacks to Liberia in Africa and Panama. Sadly, that was also a prevalent belief in the Republican Party, many of whom were former elitist Whig Party members.

As I learn more about his life, it is blatantly obvious why the historians for the Union, the winners, for some many years have wanted to hide the real Lincoln. Because of politicians like Lincoln and those that have followed him, a much greater problem has occurred. The Federal Government has now become so powerful, that it has merged the various legislative jurisdictions within the IRS Code, thus nullifying the Constitution and the rule of law, especially as it has applied to protecting the Citizens of the 50 States from Federal taxation.

Many people within the Tax Honesty Movement believe this is the primary concept the Federal Government uses to enforce the Federal Income Tax against most Americans. How they do this is, and more importantly how they get away with it, appears to be laced with fraud and corruption and has and is debated ad nauseam. The Federal Government and the IRS continue to ignore the Constitution, our own laws and our Bill of Rights.

IT'S TIME TO STOP THEM. IT'S TIME TO TAKE
ACTION AND SERVE THEM NOTICE
TO ENFORCE OUR RIGHTS.

Sources of Information/ Bibliography

1. IRS Forms: http://apps.irs.gov/app/picklist/list/formsPublications.html?indexOfFirstRow=0&sortColumn=sortOrder&value=&criteria=&resultsPerPage=25&isDescending=false
2. Title 26: http://www.law.cornell.edu/uscode/text/26
3. Government Printing Office:
http://www.gpo.gov/help/about_united_states_code.htm
4. THE FINANCIAL MANAGEMENT SERVICE is a bureau of the United States Department of the Treasury:
http://www.fms.treas.gov/index.html
5. We The People Foundation and Congress: http://www.givemeliberty.org/
6. Internal Revenue Service (IRS): http://www.irs.gov/
7. United States Department of the Treasury: http://www.irs.gov/
8. National Archives: http://www.archives.gov/federal-register/publications/statutes.html
9. Library of Congress: http://www.loc.gov/law/help/guide/federal/uscode.php
10. Office of the Law Revision Counsel –United States House of Representatives: Positive Law - http://uscodebeta.house.gov/codification/term_positive_law.htm
11. The Terminator's (Arnold Swartzenegger's) NFTL:
http://www.examiner.com/article/irs-slaps-lien-on-arnold-schwarzenegger-for-80k-back-taxes-see-court-documents
12. Formal Petition for Redress of Grievances: http://www.givemeliberty.org/FreedomDrive/Redress/PetitionTax.htm
13. eedom Above Fortune: Website of ex-IRS Criminal Investigation Division Special Agent Joe Bannister: http://www.freedomabovefortune.com/

14. New York Times Article, "Mistrial Is Declared in Tax With-holding Case" by By David Cay Johnson, Published November 27, 2003

Bibliography

Fracke, C. (1996, April 1). Protestor, son beat Tax Evasion Charges, They avoid prison but owe IRS millions. *The Balimore Sun*, pp. Home, Collections, Tax evasion. Retrieved from http://www.nytimes.com/2003/11/27/business/mistrial-is-declared-in-tax-withholding-case.html

Johnson, D. C. (2003, November 27). Mistrial Is Declared in Tax Withholding Case. *The New Your Times*, p. Archives. Retrieved from http://www.nytimes.com/2003/11/27/business/mistrial-is-declared-in-tax-withholding-case.html

LEGAL DISCLAIMER

I am not a Lawyer.
I am not a Certified Public Accountant
I am not an Enrolled Agent.
DO NOT TAKE MY WORD
FOR ANYTHING IN THIS BOOK.
Do the research and look it up for yourself.

The analysis, claims and opinions in this book are the sole observations and conclusions of the author Harry K. "Skip" Robinson and should not be relied upon as legal advice, as he is not a lawyer/Attorney. The author has tried his best at making the very complex issues of taxation understandable to those that have not studied the laws, our foundation of the rule of law and the Constitution of the United States of America. The various NFTLs used in this book were all from either Public Records or web searches on articles and/or presentations by tax professionals in dealing with the IRS. The internet is a wonderful thing. We thank you Al Gore!!!! Lol

www.ingramcontent.com/pod-product-compliance
Lightning Source LLC
Chambersburg PA
CBHW070810180526
45168CB00002B/559